A KANSAS ADVENTURE

*Watercolour of the Whitworth Farm near Emporia in the 1890s,
by John Whitworth.*

A KANSAS ADVENTURE

WHITWORTH FAMILY LETTERS FROM THE PRAIRIE

1884–1896

edited by

JANE M. RENFREW

Grosvenor House
Publishing Limited

This book is published by
Grosvenor House Publishing Ltd
Link House
140 The Broadway, Tolworth, Surrey, KT6 7HT.
www.grosvenorhousepublishing.co.uk

A CIP record for this book
is available from the British Library

ISBN 978-1-83975-632-0

DEDICATION

To the memory of John and Marian Whitworth, my great-grandparents, with admiration for their enterprise, determination and courage. Also in affectionate memory of their children May, John (my grandfather), Daisy, Walter and Gladys, and of Helen Whitworth who coped so admirably in times of adversity.

Whitworth   *Haworth*

Family crests

THE KANSAS EMIGRANTS

We cross the prairie as of old
The pilgrims crossed the sea,
To make the West, as they the East,
The homestead of the free.

We go to rear a wall of men
On Freedom's southern line,
And plant beside the cotton-tree
The rugged northern pine.

We're flowing from our native hills
As our free rivers flow;
The blessing of our Mother-land
Is on us as we go.

We go to plant her common schools
On distant prairie swells,
And give the Sabbaths of the wild
The music of her bells.

Upbearing as the Ark of old,
The bible in our van,
We go to test the truth of God
Against the fraud of man.

No pause, nor rest, save where the streams
That feed the Kansas run,
Save where our pilgrim gonfalon
Shall flout the setting sun.

We'll tread the prairie as of old
Our fathers sailed the sea,
And make the West, as they the East,
The homestead of the free.

J. G. Whittier (1807–1892)

FOREWORD

In 1991 Senator Bob Dole, Senator for Kansas, read an early draft of these letters and sent me the following letter which he kindly said could be used as a foreword to this book.

BOB DOLE
UNITED STATES SENATE

January 15, 1991

Dear Mrs. Renfrew,

Your manuscript documenting the hardships and challenges your family faced as pioneers in Kansas is poignant - and another important chapter in the history of the Western frontier.

The Whitworth family's letters graphically depict the risks and hard work of providing for a young family, as well as the joys of life on the prairie. Your moving stories reenforce for many of us the fortitude of our ancestors who were determined to conquer the vast and challenging expanses of Kansas and the West. I am particularly touched by the sensitive and compassionate passages in the letters from Emporia.

This comprehensive volume deserves careful review by serious scholars, in addition to offering a lively and readable account of bravery and adventure.

Sincerely,

BOB DOLE
United States Senate
Kansas

ACKNOWLEDGEMENTS

It is a pleasure to acknowledge my gratitude to a large number of people who have made this book possible. First my thanks must go to the late Miss Eileen Rogers and to Mrs Joan Whitworth who had inherited and carefully kept the letters from Emporia, and other family letters used in the Introduction and Postscript chapters, as well as many of the family photographs and other documentation of this episode of the family history. Other letters, documents and photographs were kept by my aunts the late Mrs Julia Carter, and the late Miss Joan Whitworth. Miss Whitworth also spent a great deal of time researching the earlier Whitworth family background in Manchester, Fleetwood, Drogheda and London. The late Mrs Marian Campin and the late Lady Talbot helped with the Whitworth and Haworth family trees. The late Mr Richard Whitworth gave details about his family in the Argentine. My husband came with me to Emporia in April 1984 when we visited the site of the Whitworth farm and the graves of my great grandparents John and Marian Whitworth. The late Mrs Gayle Graham of the Lyon County Historical Society took a great deal of trouble to provide me with further information on the Whitworths while in Kansas. She took us to the Land Registry and Record Office in Emporia where the staff were most helpful. She also arranged for us to meet Mr Robert Korte whose family had bought the farm from the Whitworths in 1896, and to visit the site of the farm and the Maplewood Cemetery. Miss Norma Redeker of Tucson, Arizona gave me details of the farmhouse, where her mother was brought up. Mr Robert Korte has drawn plans of the arrangement of rooms in the house as he remembered it from his childhood. All quotations from the *Emporia Gazette* and the *Emporia Daily Republican* are taken from the Gilson Newspaper Cuttings Scrapbook in the Lyon County Historical Museum, Emporia. The late Mrs Moira Corcoran, the late Sir Edward Gordon-Jones, Martin Ramsbottom, Mrs C. Rothwell and Miss Kay Wright have all helped me with details of the Whitworth and Haworth families, for which I am most grateful. Over the years when I have been putting this book together I have had very valuable discussions with Professor Charlotte Erickson, Dr Trebilcock, Dr Zara Steiner, the late Lady Marie Howie and Mrs Malcolm Weiner. To all these people and to many others who have encouraged me and made helpful suggestions I am extremely grateful. Mrs Jacquie Wilson typed the first version of this book, which was most helpful. Bob Dole, formerly Senator for Kansas, has kindly agreed to let me use his letter to me about the text of this book as a Foreword. My special thanks are due to those who prepared the book for publication: Greg. Matthews who scanned the illustrations, John Lowe who took so much trouble over the family trees, and above all to Anne Chippindale who put it all together so beautifully. Lastly, but by no means least, I must acknowledge the support of my family, and their great patience over the years it has taken me to reconstruct this episode in our family history.

CONTENTS

List of Illustrations

LIST OF THE LETTERS

Date	Location	From	To	Relationship
12 Feb 1873	Memphis	John Whitworth	Jane Whitworth	Sister
15 Jul 1876	Alderley Edge	John Whitworth	Jane Whitworth	Mother
24 Jul 1876	Bowdon	Marian Haworth	Jane Whitworth	prospective Mother-in-law
15 Jul 1878	Alderley Edge	Marian Whitworth	Jane Whitworth	Mother-in-law
21 Jul 1884	Manchester	John Whitworth	Jane Whitworth	Mother
19 Oct 1884	Blue Springs, Nebraska	John Whitworth	Jane Whitworth	Mother
18 Nov 1884	Emporia, Kansas	John Whitworth	Jane Whitworth	Mother
1 Dec 1884	"	"	"	"
25 Dec 1884	"	"	"	"
22 Mar 1885	"	"	"	"
23 Apl 1885	"	"	"	"
17 Aug 1885	"	"	"	"
9 Oct 1885	"	"	Benjamin Whitworth	Father
15 Dec 1885	"	"	Jane Whitworth	Mother
9 Jun 1886	"	"	Thomas Whitworth	Brother
16 Dec 1886	"	"	Jane Whitworth	Mother
26 Mar 1887	RMS *Republic* New York	"	"	"
24 Apl 1887	Emporia, Kansas	"	"	Mother
3 May 1887	"	Marian Whitworth	Abraham Haworth	Brother

Date	Location	From	To	Relationship
10 May 1887	"	John Whitworth	Jane Whitworth	Mother
10 May 1887	"	Marian Whitworth	Jesse Haworth	Brother
16 May 1887	"	"	Jane Whitworth	Mother-in-law
19 Jun 1887	"	"	Marianne Haworth	Sister-in-law
21 Aug 1887	"	"	Helena Whitworth	Sister-in-law
2 Sep 1887	"	"	Marianne Haworth	Mother
undated		Mary Whitworth	Jane Whitworth	Grandmother
18 Sep 1887	"	John Whitworth	Jane Whitworth	Mother
18 Sep 1887	Bowdon, Cheshire	Walter Haworth	Marian Whitworth	Sister
9 Oct 1887	Emporia, Kansas	Marian Whitworth	Marianne Haworth	Sister-in-law
19 Oct 1887	"	"	Jane Whitworth	Mother-in-law
25 Oct 1887	"	John & Marian Whitworth	"	Mother
29 Dec 1887	"	John Whitworth	Jane Whitworth	"
15 Jan 1888	Emporia, Kansas	Marian Whitworth	Marianne Haworth	Sister-in-law
17 Jan 1888		Marian Whitworth	Jane Whitworth	Mother-in-law
25 Jan 1888	"	"	"	"
6 Mar 1888	"	John & Marian Whitworth	"	Mother
18 Apl 1888	"	"	"	"
17 May 1888	"	Mary Whitworth	"	Grandmother
16 Aug 1888	"	Marian Whitworth	Bessie Whitworth	Sister-in-law

Date	Location	From	To	Relationship
20 Jan 1890	Manchester	Walter Haworth	Marian Whitworth	Sister
1 Oct 1890	Bowdon	"	Mary Whitworth	Niece
19 Nov 1890	Emporia, Kansas	Marian Whitworth	Marianne Haworth	Sister-in-law
28 Sept 1893	"	John Whitworth	Jane Whitworth	Mother
28 Sept 1893	"	"	Mary Boyd	Sister
28 Sept 1893	"	Marian Whitworth	Helena & Bessie Whitworth	Sisters-in-law
2 Oct 1893		Robert Whitworth	John William Stuart	Friend of family
16 Apl 1894	"	"	Abraham Haworth	Brother
24 May 1894	"	John Whitworth	Miss Thompson	Friend of family
10 Jun 1894	"	"	Helena Whitworth	Sister
24 Jul 1894	"	John Haworth Whitworth	Mary Boyd	Aunt
Sept 1894	RMS *Britannic*	Helen Whitworth	Hilda Whitworth	Sister
20 Sep 1894	Emporia, Kansas	"	Mary Boyd	Aunt
Oct 1894	"	"	Hilda Whitworth	Sister
24 Oct 1894	"	"	Helena Whitworth	Aunt
13 Nov 1894	"	"	Hilda Whitworth	Sister
Nov/Dec 1894	"	"	"	"
Nov/Dec 1894	"	"	"	"
5 Jan 1895	"	"	Bessie Whitworth	Aunt
4 Apl 1895	"	"	Hilda Whitworth	Sister
4 May 1895	"	"	"	"
4 May 1895	"	Gladys Whitworth	"	Cousin

Date	Location	From	To	Relationship
31 May 1895	"	Helen Whitworth	Jane Bryning	Aunt
2 Jun 1895	"	"	Hilda Whitworth	Sister
29 Jun 1895	"	"	"	"
12 Jul 1895	Far Creek, Kansas	"	"	"
Oct 1895	418 Exchange St, Emporia, Kansas	Helen Whitworth	Hilda Whitworth	Sister
Oct/Nov 1895	"	"	"	"
2 Nov 1895	"	"	Helena & Bessie Whitworth	Aunts
16 Nov 1895	"	"	Hilda Whitworth	Sister
18 Nov 1895	"	"	"	"
10 Dec 1895	"	"	"	"
7 Jan 1896	418 Exchange St, Emporia, Kansas	Helen Whitworth	Hilda Whitworth	Sister
Jan 1896	"	"	"	"
25 Jan 1896	"	"	Helena Whitworth	Aunt
Jan 1896	"	"	Elizabeth Whitworth	Mother
8 Mar 1896	"	"	Hilda Whitworth	Sister
22 Apl 1896	Emporia, Kansas	John Whitworth	Keystone Palace Car Co, The Rookery, Chicago	
7 May 1896	Manchester	Whitworth Telegram	Helen Whitworth	
7 May 1896	"	Haworth Telegram	"	
2 May 1896	Greenbank, Waterloo	Elizabeth Whitworth	"	Daughter

Date	Location	From	To	Relationship
9 May 1896	Emporia, Kansas	Helen Whitworth	Hilda Whitworth	Sister
2 Jun 1896	"	"	"	"
8 Jul 1896	"	"	"	"
Aug 1896	"	"	"	"
Aug 1896	"	"	"	"
Aug 1896	"	"	"	"
14 Dec 1896	Woodside, Bowdon	Jesse Haworth	Captain L. Heritage	
16 Feb 1919	Emporia, Kansas	M.B. Frith	Mary Whitworth	Friend
16 Feb 1919	"	"	J. Harvey Frith	"
22 Oct 1907	Estacion Quiroga FCO, Argentina	Walter Whitworth	Daisy Whitworth	Sister
21 May 1908	La Lornita, Berutti FCO	"	"	"
2 Feb 1909	"	"	"	"
c. 1910	"	"	Daisy Thew	"
3 Nov 1918	Keating PO, B.C. Canada	Nellie Kirkpatrick	Mary Whitworth	Nursemaid
19 Nov 1908	Emporia, Kansas	M. B. Frith	Mary Whitworth	Friend
Apl 1942	Cambridge, England	Gladys Mackennal	W. A. White	
18 Apl 1942	*Emporia Gazette*	W. A. White	Gladys Mackennal	
20 Mar 1898	Emporia, Kansas	Anne Graham	Helen Whitworth	Friend
4 Mar 1917	*en route* for France	John H. Whitworth	Helen Rogers *née* Whitworth	Cousin
16 Nov 1917	France	"	"	"
11 Apl 1918	Hale, Cheshire	Helen Rogers	Mary Whitworth	"
14 Oct 1902	31, Esmerelda, Buenos Aires, Argentina	Nicholas Whitworth	"	"

Signatures of the main correspondents:

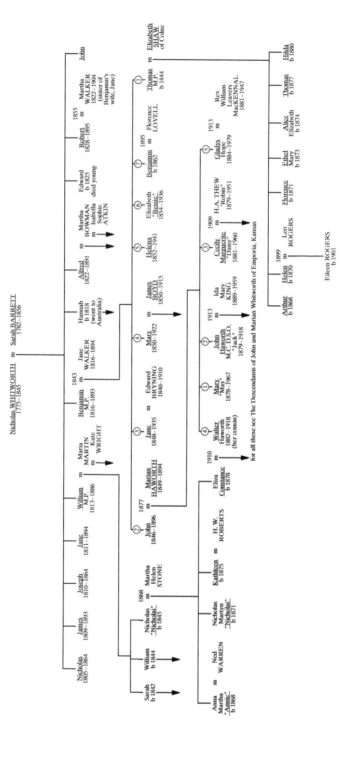

Whitworth Family Tree
(Those underlined are mentioned in the text)

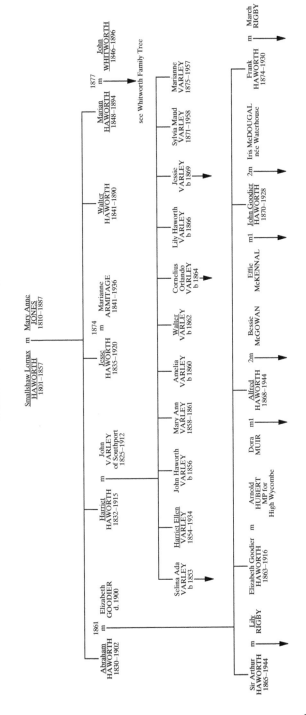

Haworth Family Tree
(Those underlined are mentioned in the text)

INTRODUCTION

Benjamin Whitworth, MP and his wife Jane Whitworth née Walker

One day, when I was a child doing a jigsaw puzzle map of the United States of America, my mother pointed to Kansas and told me that her grandparents had settled there in the Mid West at the end of last century, that they had died there, and that her father and his brother and sisters had returned to England when they were still quite young. I heard no more about this chapter in the Whitworth family history until as an undergraduate at Cambridge University I saw a good deal of my great aunt, Mrs Gladys Mackennal, who lived in Cambridge. She was the youngest of the children who had returned from Kansas, and as she grew older she often used to reminisce about the freedom and exploits of her childhood in the Mid West. When I told her that I would like to write about it she said it was a story which ought to be told. She died in May 1979, and among her papers was the watercolour of the farm which appears as the frontispiece.

It was not, however, until the discovery in 1980 of two bundles of letters tied up with ribbons in the attic of Miss Eileen Rogers's home in Ashbourne, Derbyshire, that the details of this remarkable story began to come into sharp focus. They were the letters of my great grandfather John Whitworth and his wife Marian, tied up in two separate bundles. They had been sent from Kansas to John's parents Benjamin and Jane, and to his elder brother Thomas, and to his sisters Helena, Bessie and Jane. They had clearly been valued and carefully saved by the recipients, as being of special interest. Indeed, one of the letters to Thomas had been printed in a Manchester newspaper as being of special interest to

1

those who might think of settling in Kansas. Eileen Rogers also had a collection of letters sent back by her mother Helen, the eldest daughter of Thomas Whitworth, who had gone out later to help her uncle and cousins on the farm near Emporia. These letters were mainly written to Helen's younger sister, Hilda. When I put these together in chronological order they made a fascinating story, but there were gaps. Enquiries round the family revealed more letters had survived. By good fortune Mrs Joan Whitworth, widow of Air Commodore John H. Whitworth, found that she had letters which filled some of the gaps; they included letters from Marian Whitworth to her own family, the Haworths, and a few letters from them to her. They had been given to Mary (May) Whitworth, the oldest of the children to return from Kansas, and from her they passed down to her nephew John. Mrs Joan Whitworth also had a good series of photographs of the Kansas farm. My aunts, the late Mrs Julia Carter and the late Miss Joan Whitworth also had a few letters, some documents and quite a collection of photographs which had belonged to my grandfather, John Haworth Whitworth. A visit to Emporia, Kansas, in 1984, with my husband, located information about the acquisition of land, and the census return of 1895. From this I have been able to piece together this remarkable story of optimism, enterprise, bravery and true British grit in the face of enormous adversity.

Just imagine. Having been brought up in a comparatively well-to-do family, working in the Cotton Exchange in Manchester in a relatively stable job, but not one he enjoyed, John Whitworth was faced with the situation that his family fortunes were much diminished and he needed to stretch his income to cover the expenses of supporting a young family with five children. He took the decision to leave his job, his family and friends, to take his limited capital and to settle in the Mid West of America and start farming, for which he had no previous experience, but a love of horses and of the outdoor life. Why did John choose America? We don't know for sure. There had been family connections in the previous generations. His grandfather Nicholas Whitworth (1775–1845), who was a corn merchant in Manchester and an active radical, had taken his young family to Philadelphia after the Peterloo Massacre in Manchester in 1819. He returned four years later and settled in Drogheda. His fifth son, Benjamin (1816–1893), who had worked his way up in the cotton trade from being apprenticed to a fustian manufacturer on leaving school at 16, became a successful and wealthy businessman engaged in importing raw cotton from America for his mills in Lancashire and Drogheda. His business was severely hit by the American Civil War, which cut off this important source of supply in the 1860s, and by a number of misfortunes at the end of the 1870s. Benjamin was also interested in politics, like his father, and became MP for Drogheda 1865–68, for Kilkenny 1875–1880, and again for Drogheda 1880–1885.

John Whitworth was Benjamin's second son. He was born in 1846 in Altrincham, Cheshire, and was brought up in Fleetwood on the Lancashire coast, where his father had moved on doctor's advice in 1849. The family moved back to Manchester in 1862, first to Irwell House, Drinkwater Park, Prestwich, and then in 1866 to Outrington Hall, Lymm. In 1868 Benjamin and his wife Jane moved to London, and this was to be their home for the rest of their lives. John had quite a different character from his father and grandfather; he was not interested in business, public affairs or politics. He was a keen sportsman enjoying the outdoor life, an excellent shot, an expert horseman and a powerful swimmer. He frequently rode his own horses in the show ring and also had a special skill in breaking in and managing horses. He would have made a country squire, but fate was to decree otherwise. After his schooling he joined the family firm of cotton brokers in Manchester, working at the Cotton Exchange together with his elder brother, Thomas. He took little part in public affairs in Manchester, apart from being actively concerned with the management of the Heyrod Street Mission in Ancoats with Mr William O'Hanlon. This mission has been described as 'an oasis of healing springs in the peopled desert of Ancoats'; Mr William O'Hanlon was a leading member of the Bowdon Downs Congregational church, and he recruited other members of that congregation to help him with this mission.

It was his work in cotton dealing which first took John Whitworth to America in September 1872, in an effort to re-establish contacts with the cotton suppliers after the end of the American Civil War. He travelled across the Atlantic on the O.S.N. Co.'s steamer Adriatic, leaving Liverpool on Thursday 29th August. He travelled with a group of friends which included Walter Haworth, who kept a diary of the trip. The voyage was uneventful; Walter Haworth describes a typical day: 'Breakfast (8.30) then walk, talk, smoke, drink, flirt (if opportunity serves), bet and gamble about anything ... till lunch (1pm), then repeat the foregoing till dinner (6pm). After this, walking deck by moonlight, singing, recitations and suchlike till bedtime. One night we had a long drawn out lecture on Egypt by an American clergyman – he managed thereby to send us off to roost a little earlier than usual'. They landed in New York on Sunday 8th September 1872, and the whole party of friends, Whitworth, Hodgkinson, Hardie, Coghill, Heyworth, Matthew and Walter Haworth all spent the night at the St Nicholas Hotel before going their separate ways. John Whitworth went to Memphis and it was here that he was visited by Walter Haworth on 10th October. The next day they saw 'cotton bought, sold, branded, packed etc (wrote Walter Haworth in his diary) and now I feel I know a little more of the article I so often talk about. Have also visited the fields and seen it in its pristine glory'. Walter Haworth bade a fond farewell to 'Mr John' before leaving on 12th October to return by easy stages to England.

Re-establishing trade contacts was not all hard work, as the following letter from John to his sister Jane shows. Family tradition also maintains that he impressed his American friends by swimming across the Mississippi River.

Memphis Feby 12th 1873

Dear Jane

I received your letter yesterday and was glad to hear that Mother was going to Spain as the Out will do her good. Mary must be having a nice time of it in Manchester. Do not approve of younger sisters going out of their turn. I have been having some good fun here lately having been introduced to some of the nicest girls here. I have been taking them turn about to concerts. You ask the lady to go with you, call for her in a carriage, and after the concert take her back. You may know a girl here 12 months and never see her Father, or Mother, or Brother, unless one of them sits up to open the door. I took a very pretty young lady last night to a concert. Rubenstein, the finest pianist in the world, a first class violinist and Leibhart being the three stars. You do lots of things here that would appear very cheeky in England. I was introduced to a young lady from Louisville and asked her about quarter of an hour after to go to a concert with me. What would Mother say if some unknown gentleman called and asked you to go to a concert with him? In Cornhill Magazine, I believe page 206, you will find a first rate article on American customs entitled 'Some peculiarities of Society in America' you had better get it as it will amuse you greatly. Tom writes asking me to go home but I do not see my way clear to leaving the business here, so have written to him to that effect. We have done with the cold weather now, have had some warm days lately.

With best love to all, your affec. Brother,
John Whitworth

His efforts were clearly successful, as increasing numbers of shiploads of American cotton arrived in Fleetwood. In 1875 an additional large shed was erected in Adelaide Street, Fleetwood to receive the bales of cotton for Messrs B. Whitworth and Bros: in that year 33 shiploads arrived in the

John Whitworth about the
time of his marriage

Marian Haworth about the time of her
wedding to John Whitworth

port for them. He did eventually return home, but the attractions of life in America made a lasting impression on him.

Whilst working on the Cotton Exchange in Manchester he had first become acquainted with Walter Haworth who, as noted above, became quite a friend. He belonged to a family which had lived in Bolton, Lancashire in the 1830s, and then had moved to Salford about 1840 and there they had become members of the Hope Congregational Church. Another member of the church was James Dilworth who had a large cotton spinning business, and who employed the Haworth brothers in his warehouse. Walter Haworth, who had two elder brothers Abraham and Jesse and an elder sister Harriet, and also, most importantly for this story, had a younger sister Marian, who was born in 1849. It was Marian who was to become the focus of John Whitworth's affections.

She was the youngest daughter of Smallshaw Lomax Haworth and his wife Marianne, *née* Jones. Marian's father, who was related to the Hesketh and Leverhulme families, had died when she was about ten years old, having been an invalid for many years. Her mother, Marianne, apparently could neither read nor write, but in the 1870s she was living at Ecclesfield, Bowdon, and stayed there until her death in September

1887. Marian had three brothers and a sister all older than herself: Abraham (1830–1902), who eventually became head of the firm of James Dilworth & Son and who married Elizabeth Goodier (d. 1900); Harriet (1840–1915) who married John Varley, a draper of Southport; Jesse (1842–1920) who was also to become a partner in James Dilworth & Son and who married Marianne Armitage (1841–1936); and Walter (1846–1890). also a partner in James Dilworth & Son, who was unmarried, and lived at Ecclesfield with his mother and youngest sister. Marian herself was born on 14th January 1849.

John Whitworth and Marian Haworth's romance came to a head in July 1876 as the following letters explain:

Brook Villa, Alderley Edge July 15th 1876

Dear Mother,

I intend if possible to run up and see you on Tuesday night and stay at any rate over Wednesday, Tom's being juror at the Assizes may prevent my staying longer. You are no doubt aware I have long had a liking for Marian Haworth, Walter's sister, but could never see how she could leave her mother, however I thought it only fair to Marian and to myself to speak to

Opposite:
Wedding invitation for
John and Marian's
wedding, 21st June 1877;
Sketch of Bowdon Downs
Congregational Church, by
Miss Ethel Hall;
The Order of Service
This page: Menu for the
wedding breakfast at
Ecclesfield, Bowdon;
List of speeches at the
wedding breakfast;
Notice of the wedding of
John and Marian
Whitworth

Marian and settle the matter one way or the other. I did so last Saturday, but she could not see her way out of the difficulty. I told her, however, that her Mother would be pleased to see her comfortably settled before she died. Abraham spoke to Mrs Haworth on Thursday, and although dreadfully cut up, still saw the matter in its right light and offered no opposition. Marian wrote me this morning accepting my offer, consequently I rode over this afternoon and saw the old lady. She received me very kindly indeed but I could see that she was struggling hard to conceal her feelings. She has known me a long time, however, and I think has every confidence in me. As you do not know the young lady I must try and describe her to you. She is slightly taller than Jane and rather lighter built, not handsome but pleasing

7

looking, dark hair and eyes and rather short upper lip. I have not chosen her for her good looks but for her good qualities. She is a most affectionate daughter and sister, and amiable and good tempered. She is a staunch teetotaller and Dissenter and above all a Christian, so I think I have every requisite for happiness in my choice. I have felt anything but settled of late but hope I shall now. Write me kindly by return and let me know whether you and Father are satisfied by what I have done.

Your affec. son,
John Whitworth

On her engagement Marian wrote to her future mother-in-law, Jane Whitworth, as follows:

Ecclesfield, 24th July 1876

My dear Mrs Whitworth,
I hardly know how to thank you enough for your letter. It is very precious to receive such kind words and welcome from you, and members of your family, yet it makes me very humble and half fearful, lest you should have formed a false estimate of me. I trust, however, I may more than realise your wishes and that you will learn to love me not only for John's sake but my own. Mama sends her love and hopes to see you when you come north, she also wishes to be remembered to her great favourite, Bessie. Again thanking you for your letter.

With much love to you, Mr Whitworth and the girls, believe me dear Mrs Whitworth,
yrs. most affectionately,
Marian Haworth

The wedding took place eleven months later in Bowdon Downs Congregational Church, at 11 a.m. on Thursday 21st June 1877. The service was conducted by the Revd A. Mackennal (Minister, Bowdon Downs, 1876–1904) and the Revd H. Griffiths (Minister, Bowdon Downs, 1866–1876). Copies of the invitation to the wedding, the Order of Service, the menu for the Wedding Breakfast which took place at Ecclesfield, Bowdon, and the programme of toasts (an impressive number by any standard) are all illustrated here. John and Marian's wedding presents included dining-room and drawing-room clocks given to them by Jesse Haworth. (They were bought from Messrs Miller & Sons, 178/179 Piccadilly, London, in May 1877 for £63.4.6d). John's brother Thomas gave them a set of knives, and his sister Jane gave them a best china tea service.

John and Marian set up home at Brook Villa, Alderley Edge, where John had been living before his marriage, and it was here that their older children were born. The oldest was Mary (May) born in July 1878.

Brook Villa, Alderley Edge, Monday night 15 July 1878

My dear Mother,

The parcel containing Baby's cloak etc arrived quite safely this afternoon. I hardly know how to thank you, they are so very beautiful. John has been spending Sunday at Blackpool so Mama came to keep me company. She was here when the cloak and hood arrived. She says they are the handsomest she has ever seen. We dressed the baby in her grand things. I wish you could have seen her, she looked like a diminutive bride. I have just shown the things to John, he says they are simply absurd, such grandeur, do we think she is a princess? Though he talks this way, I can see he is as proud as can be of them, and does not think them one bit too grand for his darling. I am thankful to say both baby and myself are getting on famously. I have been downstairs for several days and hope to go in the carriage to see Mary tomorrow morning. We are still undecided about the name, which do you prefer Mary Carina or Mary Evelyn? I hope you have got rid of all the colds in the house. John joins me in sending love to all, and with many thanks,

Your affectionate daughter,

Marian

Mary's (May) arrival in 1878 was followed by that of John Haworth (Jack) in 1879, Cicely Marguerite (Daisy) in 1881 and Walter Haworth in 1882. By 1883 they had moved to Glebelands, Stamford Road, Bowdon, where their youngest child Gladys Hope was born in July 1884.

Even before Gladys was born, John had decided to take his limited capital and move to America, to try his luck farming in the Mid West.

Manchester, July 21/84

My dear Mother,

I hope you feel comfortable in your new house.* Tom has secured lodgings for Archer at Tom Beswick's. You remember he was cowman at

Oughtrington, so knows Archer well. I should think it would be a very suitable place for him. May is still at Miss Griffith's at Saltaire, we have very good accounts of her. She will be home about the end of the month. Jack, Daisy, and Walter keep well but would be all the better for a few days at the seaside as they still have an occasional cough and the Chicken Pox has left Daisy with a running from one ear. Marian is only very soso. I called Dr Jones in on Saturday, he thought this week would see an arrival. I do hope she will have a good time I feel very anxious about her, as she never did so badly as in the last few months.

I hope to get my business squared up and to get away by 26th next month but everything is very uncertain. Father used to have a gun, if he does not intend using it again and if Ben is not likely to want it I should be glad to have it. I have one but a spare one would be very useful out West.

Are you likely to be down our way soon or not? Business, I am sorry to say, does not brighten but it is a long road that has no turning.

Your affec. son

John

* Benjamin and Jane Whitworth moved from 11 Holland Park to 22 Daleham Gardens, Hampstead (a recently built semi-detached house) in July 1884.

Gladys Hope Whitworth arrived safely on 27th July 1884. John Whitworth left England as planned towards the end of August. He travelled by boat to New York and then by rail to Iowa and on in a covered wagon:

> To the West, to the West, to the land of the Free,
> Where the mighty Missouri rolls down to the sea;
> Where a man is a man even though he must toil
> And the poorest may gather the fruits of the soil.

[An emigration ballad sung by Andrew Carnegie's father and recalled by him in old age] (Maldwyn A. Jones, *Destination America*, 1976, p. 15)

The American Background

John Whitworth's decision to move to the Mid West in 1884 probably stemmed from the dramatic decline in the family fortunes at the end of the

1870s, and was also coloured by his enjoyable stay in Memphis in 1872/3. He may well have seen the railway companies' advertisements for cheap land in Kansas, and have been attracted by the prospect of an outdoor life which appealed to him. At home, work on the - Cotton - Exchange in Manchester did not agree with him: he suffered from bilious attacks, insomnia, some sort of skin complaint and headaches. In the less stressful open-air activities of farming these troubles disappeared.

He finally decided in the summer of 1884 to take the plunge and go out to the Mid West to look for a suitable place in which to settle, and to leave his family at home until he was well established on the farm. Marian, living in Bowdon again, close to her brothers and within easy walking distance of Ecclesfield, could keep an eye on her aged mother for a little longer as well as caring for her five young children.

Poster advertising sale of land in Kansas by the Union Pacific Railroad Co., 1867

After travelling south and west from Iowa in a covered wagon looking for a suitable place to farm, John Whitworth's choice fell on Kansas which had formed part of the Louisiana Purchase of 1803, and had been admitted to the Union as the 34th State in 1861. His selection of this particular state would certainly have met with the approval of his father and of his wife, since it had become a prohibition state by a constitutional amendment in 1880, enforced by the Murray Liquor Law in 1881, and still remains so.

The area he selected, and the farm which he bought, lay some four miles east of the town of Emporia in Lyon County, Kansas. It was located in Section 8 of Township 19, Range 12 of Lyon County. (When the new land in the West was opened up for settlement it was initially owned by the American federal government, and before it could be sold it was surveyed and divided up into a series of Ranges, six miles wide, counting from east to west. The Ranges were subdivided up into Townships, six miles square and

Map showing the land settled in the US between 1870 and 1890

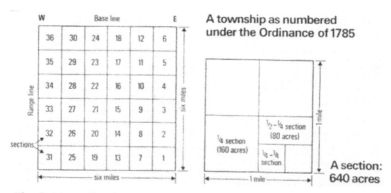

The division of land into Townships, and their sub-division into Sections as numbered under the Ordinance of 1785

numbered from south to north beginning up the east side of each Range. Each Range contained 36 Townships. The Townships were then subdivided into Sections one mile square (640 acres). These were often subdivided into quarter Sections (160 acres) or even smaller units).

Emporia had been founded on 20th February 1857 by a company of five men from Lawrence, Kansas who wanted to found a new town. They chose the site some six miles above the confluence of the Neosho and Cottonwood Rivers on 'the loveliest site in the world for a town', surveyed the four corner posts in position in the snow, and two members of the company made their way back to Lecompton to make the formal entry of the site description with the Surveyor General. On the same day the Territorial Legislative ratified the town charter for Emporia, named after a historic Greek market centre on the African coast of the Mediterranean. It was incorporated in 1870.

The first buildings were constructed on the northwest corner of Commercial Street and 6th Avenue. The State Normal College opened in 1865 with 25 students. When J.W. Truitt edited the Emporia City Directory in 1883 he wrote 'Only those who 25 years ago wended their slow and weary way across the monotonous miles (perhaps most of them by ox-cart) of open prairie from Lawrence to come upon a little frontier hamlet surrounded by vast expanses of wild prairie inhabited principally by the Indian and the buffalo, the tall grass of which switched the very sides of the houses in the young town ... can fully realise that the town of Emporia has grown to the present beautiful city.' The population of Emporia in 1880 was 4631, and by 1890 it had risen to 7551. The Atchison, Topeka and Santa Fe Railway met and crossed the Missouri Pacific Railway here. The chief industries of the town in 1883 were flour milling, an iron foundry, a water-powered furniture factory and two steam woodwork factories. There were thirteen hotels, fifteen churches, four ward public school buildings, a high school, two opera houses and a masonic temple. In 2010 Emporia had a population of 24,916; it is the county seat and largest town of Lyon County, Kansas.

The early 1880s were a boom time for the settlement of Kansas. The Kansas Board of Agriculture told prospective settlers 'Kansas agriculture means a life of ease, perpetual June weather, and a steady diet of milk and honey.' In the spring of 1885 the Lorned (Kansas) Optic reported that 'the largest immigration ever known in the history of the state is now steadily flowing into south west Kansas.' This boom spirit was encouraged by the Eastern banks and loan companies which were eager to lend money for farm mortgages in Kansas and Nebraska.

The hardworking routine of these early farmers is well summarised by Henry Steele Commager in The West (p.231): 'Hard work characterised

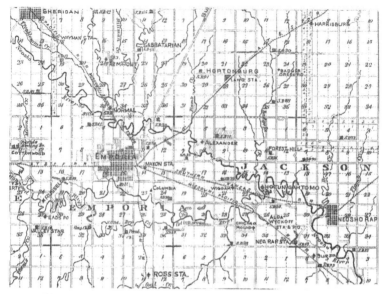

This is to certify that I have examined the plans of Lyon County and Emporia City, prepared for L. H. Everts & Co., and I believe them to be as nearly accurate as it is possible to make them. I know that great care has been taken by the Surveyor in compiling them. The map of Emporia City and surroundings is especially complete, and by far the best map of the city yet prepared. Witness my hand, and the seal of Lyon County, at Emporia, this 9th day of July, 1886.

Roland Larkin
County Clerk

Above: Map of Lyon County, Kansas, 1886; Below, detail including Emporia and the site of the Whitworth Farm

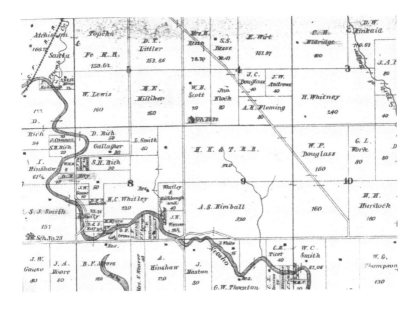

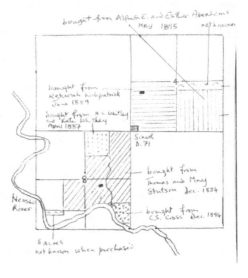

Above: Map of the area of the farm in 1878 before John Whitworth bought it, showing where some of the neighbours mentioned in the letters lived. It is taken from Edwards Brothers 1878, Township 19 South Range 12 East

Right: Diagram to show the acquisition of land for the Whitworth Farm, 1884–1896

the daily existence for most farmers and their families, as it did in most rural areas in the nineteenth century. The round of planting and harvesting, along with the usual chores connected with tending livestock, kept farmers busy from early morning till late at night during much of the year. Most of the work was dull and monotonous ... while men were in the fields housewives pursued a daily round of washing, baking, sewing, garden work (in summer), and raising children ... Women also worked in the fields, milked the cows and tended the chickens. Children too had their daily responsibilities: herding cattle, milking, gathering fuel and helping at other tasks.'

Social gatherings were held in the local towns, to which the farmer frequently travelled by buggy or wagon, especially when there was not too much work to do on the farm. There the farmers and their wives would gather in the local stores and enjoy a little sociability, and exchange news and gossip. Visits between neighbours were infrequent because of the distances between farms. The churches became the focal point for many social activities, and in rural areas services were sometimes taken in the local schools by itinerant ministers or by the local lay preacher.

Many Mid West farmers grew corn (maize) and wheat, and also oats and barley. Vegetables were grown for home consumption. Most farmers also kept livestock; cattle, sheep, pigs and some poultry. Sales of surplus butter, eggs, grain, and livestock sold in the local town were the chief sources of the family income. If the new farmer had good crops and his livestock kept free from disease for the first few seasons, he was more likely to succeed as this gave him a chance to build up his capital reserves before calamities such as drought or plagues of grasshoppers might strike. It was important that he should know which crops and animals would succeed on his land, and what combination would be the most profitable. Water was a vital commodity on the prairies. In many places water was obtained from wells often only 10 m deep. Water was drawn to the surface in buckets, by hand, or by pump, until the farmer could afford a windmill. The wind pump made use of the constant prairie winds to raise a constant supply of water, enough for the farmer's needs, and those of his household, but not enough to irrigate the crops.

Maize (corn) was the chief cereal crop grown in Kansas in the 1880s. The difficulty was that the hot dry winds of July and August usually burned and destroyed the crop, and in most years the rainfall was inadequate. After the severe droughts in the late 1880s Kansas farmers changed to cultivating wheat as their main grain crop. Farmers on the plains also relied increasingly on livestock which were less susceptible to drought conditions, and a combination of livestock and drought resistant crops was the most successful. As the farms became more established they also became more mechanized: cultivators, mowing machines, hayrakes, grain drills, seeders, corn planters and threshing machines became common. But even in 1890 the ordinary prairie farmer had less than $500 worth of machinery.

Farmers in the Mid West also paid higher interest rates than those in the Eastern States: it was common to pay anything between 8 and 12 percent interest on real estate mortgages in the 1870s and 1880s and for loans on machinery and livestock interest of as much as 2/3 percent a month was charged. One Nebraska farmer wrote in 1890 that the state had three crops: 'a crop of corn, a crop of freight charges and a crop of interest.' Initially most farmers owned their own land but in the 1870s and 1880s an increasing number mortgaged their farms to obtain operating capital. Then, when unable to meet principal and interest payments, thousands of farmers lost their land through foreclosure. Between 1889 and 1893 some 11,000 mortgages were foreclosed in Kansas alone.

Unfortunately the optimism of the early 1880s was not altogether based on reality: the new farmers were soon faced by rising costs and falling prices, made worse by the rapid agricultural expansion in the Mid-West. Hopes of prosperity were based on 'unrealistic assumptions about the land, the weather, the market and the credit system.' Added to this was the absolute dependence on the railways and their freight charges for marketing the surplus produce. Moreover the prices charged for daily necessities – furniture, clothing, lumber and leather goods were kept high by the operation of protective price tariffs. The new settlers in the West found that farming yielded decreasing returns as well as social isolation.

The isolation on the farmstead was terrible, and it was probably the women that felt it most. 'The farmer's wife had to be mother, mistress, nurse, seamstress, doctor, cook, comforter and teacher ... it was she who first acquired the symbols of respectability – the dignity of a pony and trap, a frame house, and such high-toned city amenities as wallpaper, carpets, pictures on the wall, an organ or a piano ... it was the mother who accompanied the family hymn singing and read books aloud, especially the "Good Book"' (A. Cooke, p. 238). It was a hard and lonely life as reflected in these lines of Stephen Vincent Benét's John Vilas:

> *I took my wife out of a pretty house,*
> *I took my wife out of a pleasant place,*
> *I stripped my wife of pleasant things,*
> *I drove my wife to wander with the wind.*

John Brown's Body, Book III

The immigrant farmer in Kansas in the 1880s was subjected to the devastating effects of deflation following the land boom. The climate also dealt a fairly disastrous blow to prosperity: after several years of excessive rainfall, the summer of 1887 was so dry that crops withered in the fields. Eight of the next ten years were extremely arid, especially in western Kansas, and the area also suffered from plagues of grasshoppers, cinch bugs, prairie fires, high winds, tornadoes, blizzards, hail and killing frosts. The conditions were so extreme that half the population of western Kansas deserted the country between 1888 and 1892. Conditions were even worse in 1894, the driest summer on record up to that time, when only 8 or 9 inches of rain fell during the year on large areas of the plains; thousands of farmers experienced total and complete crop failure. The district around Emporia was not so badly affected but nonetheless the newly immigrated farmer cannot have found it encouraging to see so many settlers returning to the Eastern States with 'In God we trusted: in Kansas we busted' scrawled on the sides of their wagons.

The long-term effect of the agricultural depression which began in 1887 was a major economic crisis. Both the farmers and the railway companies were hit severely and American trade oversees was also affected by business distress in Europe and Australia. By mid summer 1893 the panic was in full swing with the failure of the Reading, Erie and Northern Pacific Railroads, and the Union Pacific and Santa Fé railway companies were in the hands of the receivers. Banks too began to fail: there were 158 national bank failures in 1893, 153 of them in the Southern and Western States. By the summer of 1894 there were four million unemployed in the cities and towns vainly looking for work. A special session of Congress which repealed the Sherman Silver Purchase Act of 1890 was summoned by President Cleveland. However, this did not succeed in raising the price of silver, increasing the amount of money in circulation or in halting the steady decline in crop prices. Once free of the obligation to buy silver, the Treasury was subjected to a run on its gold reserves, and it was not until after four successive issues of bonds for gold – the last in 1896 – that the crisis really passed.

Nevertheless, despite all their problems and difficulties, even before the turn of the century, plains farmers had added greatly to the nation's growing agricultural production, and thus played an important role in the economic development of the United States.

Although, as it turned out, the background events during the years when the Whitworth family lived in Kansas were not at all auspicious, yet they were determined to make a success of their venture, come what may. In the event it was tragic family circumstances, not outside forces, which led to the end of this chapter in the Whitworth family story. The story that follows is largely told through the letters they sent home to the family in England which give a vivid picture of life on the Kansas prairie in the late nineteenth century.

Marian Whitworth and the children left behind in England

Bibliography of the Introduction

S.V. Benét, 1928: *John Brown's Body,* Doubleday Doran, Garden City

D. Brown, 1995: *The American West,* Simon and Schuster, New York

H.S. Commager, M. Cunliffe and M.A. Jones, 1980: *The West, an Illustrated History,* Orbis Publishing Co., London

A. Cooke, 1973: *Alistair Cooke's America,* Alfred Knopf, New York

Edwards Brothers of Missouri, 1878: *An Illustrated Historical Atlas of Lyon County, Kansas,* Philadelphia

M. Johnson, 1985: *The Wild West,* Treasure Press, London

M.A. Jones, 1976: *Destination America,* Fontana and Thames Television, London

C.A. Milner II, C.A. O'Connor and M.A. Sandweiss, 1994: *The Oxford History of the American West,* Oxford University Press, Oxford

S.E. Morrison, H.S. Commager and W.E. Leuchtenberg, 1983: *Concise History of the American Republic* (2nd edition), Oxford University Press, Oxford

Schools Council History 13–16 Project, 1977: *The American West 1840–1895,* Holmes McDougall Ltd, Edinburgh

J.W. Truitt, 1883: *Emporia City Directory*

THE LETTERS
PART I

1884–1887

Blue Springs. Oct 19 1884

My dearest Mother,

I have been longing to drop you a line for some time but as I have been camping out for the last fortnight I have had neither the time nor the opportunity to write. I bought two good horses in Iowa and have been travelling in a covered wagon. At night we put up a tent and feel as comfortable as possible. I have done all the cooking so far, no joke when you have to fetch the water from some distance and then collect sufficient sticks for a fire. We have very little rain in winter in this country, and have only had one wet night since we set out. I bought a pretty little fox terrier out with me but unfortunately it got run over by the wagon and I had to bury her in a cornfield. I like this country very much but the worst feature is the scarcity of servants. A servant won't stop unless she has her meals with the family, the only plan is to bring one out with you. England is no doubt the most comfortable place in the world if you have plenty of money but as far as I can see money will go twice as far here as in England. Clothes are dear but no one wears any; I don't mean that they go about like Adam and Eve but they wear their clothes in rags before they replace them. Weather today 84 in the shade, trousers and shirt ample clothing. I am feeling really well and have an appetite like a horse. I am writing this at Mr Fenton's house in southern Nebraska where we have been staying for 3 or 4 days. Tomorrow we set out for Kansas. I like this neighbourhood very much and if I don't find Kansas as nice I shall return to it. I miss Marian and the children dreadfully, still I could not do with them here until I got settled. They have a splendid corn harvest; I plucked one ear with 950 grains on it. Food is very cheap here but labour scarce and dear.

Your affec. Son,
John.

Emporia Nov 18 1884

My dear Mother,

I dare say you have often wondered how I have been getting on over here. For about five weeks we camped out wherever 5 o'clock found us. The life has suited me admirably. I weigh nearly a stone heavier than when I left home, and am as brown as Father when he comes home from his Irish fishing trips. I like this country very much and think Kansas a nice healthy place. I have made up my mind to settle somewhere about here and have seen several places I like very much but have not yet made a final decision. The only thing against this country is the distance from one's friends and acquaintances. Up to Saturday we had glorious weather but yesterday it suddenly turned cold and has been snowing all day. We may have lots of beautiful weather yet before Christmas after that we expect one or two cold snaps of a day or two each with temperatures down to 20 below zero, but winter will be over by the middle of February. I have met very few Englishmen down here but a good many have settled all around if one only looked them up. People are rushing into Kansas at an enormous rate. The State gained 10% in population last year. Land is worth double what it could have been bought at two years ago and every sign it is going to go much higher. People are beginning to find out that the Western States are pleasanter to live in than the Eastern and land is only half the value. This is certainly the spot for anyone who has only small capital, any one with ready money can buy to great advantage. Farmers think nothing of paying 15% to 20% for temporary loans, mortgaging their horses and cattle to secure it. I miss Marian and the little ones dreadfully. I would give anything to have little Walter here for half an hour, the baby I shall not know when I do see it. I think this country will suit Marian and the children very well indeed as the air is light and exhilarating being about 1,100 feet above sea level, the only trouble is that servants cannot be obtained. She will have to bring one out. A lady help would be very useful if she could only find the right one. The men here look very well but the women don't, I think they take sadly too little outdoor exercise and many of them are sadly overworked. This state is a great State for cattle and that is what I intend going in for as it needs fewer men and gives less trouble in the house. Nearly all the houses are made of wood with stone cellars. Please give my love to all and I should like to hear from you occasionally, letters addressed to J & J Stuart & Co., Nassau Street, New York, will find me.

Your affec. Son,
John.

Emporia Dec 1st 1884

My dear Mother,

I daresay you often wonder how I am getting along over here, I know that I often wonder how you all are. Kansas has a splendid climate, today is cool but a beautifully clear blue sky and plenty of sunshine makes it delightful. I am doing nothing for the moment except to look after and exercise my two horses. I have seen several farms and hope to get settled in a week or two. I am sure I shall like this country very much when I can get Marian and the children around me again, but the finest country in the world would seem a desert without them. Fruit grows luxuriously; apples, pears, grapes, figs, peaches, apricots, plums, mulberries, gooseberries and a host of others. The summers are hot but are always bearable as the wind blows almost constantly in this prairie country and the nights are always cool and comfortable. The winter so far has been grand and the autumn delightful. I feel certain I shall get along first rate here, lots of chances for anyone with little capital and plenty of energy and pluck. Marian seems to think that she is coming out to a howling wilderness where the children cannot be properly educated, but the schools in this town are first class and very cheap. The finest buildings in all this western country are the school houses and colleges. The Ministers here would compare very favourably with any in England. Kansas is only about thirty years old, another 10 will see every yard of ground occupied as settlers are coming in by thousands. I have left the hotel and taken a very nicely furnished front room which I use both for sitting room and bedroom. It is lonely work, I would infinitely rather be at work on the farm. The children will enjoy this country immensely, especially if they should be as fond of animals as I used to be. I only wish I had come out to this country 10 years ago, land could then have been bought for one fourth its present price. I often wish all our friends and relatives were here, though what father would do I cannot tell, the quiet country life suits me exactly. I feel quite a new man. I suppose as I have heard nothing to the contrary all our relatives are well, get one of the girls to write to me occasionally. With love to all.

Your affec. Son,
John.

Emporia Christmas Day 1884

My dear Mother,
Your letter from Bowdon reached me this afternoon, mails are not coming through very quickly and I don't wonder at it as we have had a very heavy fall of snow. We are having 43 degrees of frost this far south, north they have had it down to 43 below zero or 75 degrees of frost. I have done nothing the past 10 days but feed my horses and keep the stove warm. I don't feel cold particularly except when it blows. I am glad to hear such good reports of Marian and the children. I would give a good deal for a peep at little Walter, he was always Daddy's boy. I am very sorry to hear such bad reports of Tom, I feel sure I could not have stood the great anxiety many months longer without breaking down. I keep first class and am getting quite stout. I told two friends at dinner that it was my birthday they guessed I was 35. I have bought a nice farm 4 miles from here, it has the makings of a lovely spot, plenty of nice timber and nice limpid streams and two fine orchards, all kinds of fruit grow splendidly

here. I intend putting in 2 or 3 hundred vines this spring. The longer I stay here the better I like it, life does not seem as full as at home. The one great trouble is being so far from you all. This western country is growing in the most marvellous manner simply by leaps and bounds. I had a dreadfully quiet birthday and Christmas Day, this morning I went to church and have been reading in my room all afternoon. I have just made tea and washed up and then sat down to answer your letter.

I expect to be hard at work on my farm in about 3 weeks from now. Weather at present too cold to do any outside work. I have not been able even to exercise my horses for 10 days. Cold seldom lasts long here, probably my next letter may advise beautiful weather. No fogs here, atmosphere always clear and light. I have not had a headache since I came. Marian tells me neither her brother Walter nor George Massey are at all well, that Exchange work takes it out of one dreadfully. I would not go back to it on any account. I value health far more than money. I hope business will soon take a turn for the better. Here I have no complaints, everything very cheap, rabbits selling wholesale at 2d each.

Your affec. Son,
John.

He bought his farm from Thomas J. and Mary Anne Stutson of Madison County, Ohio, together with about 200 acres of surrounding farmland beside the Neosho River some 4 miles east of Emporia. It lies in Section 8 of Township 19, Range 12, of Lyon County, Kansas. He paid $8,000 for all this property. The Mortgage record for Lyon County records that on 26 January 1885 John and Marian Whitworth mortgaged the property to Abraham Haworth (Marian's elder brother) for $8,000. The Mortgage was paid off in full on 12 September 1896.

Emporia March 22 1885

My dear Mother,

It seems a long time since I heard from any of you, suppose you are getting along much as usual. We are having a very late Spring hard frosts every night and plenty of high winds but we have now reached the time of year when we may expect some lovely weather. We have had a foretaste of it already. Everything seems to be working nicely and the farm keeps one busily occupied all the time. We have not yet been able to do any ploughing, ground being soft and wet. Indian corn is a great crop here grows 8 or 10 feet tall. I am feeding my cattle largely on sugar cane, they seem to do well on it. I intend planting a good deal of it this Spring. I like this climate better than England, air seems so exhilarating I never longed for my meals so much in my life. I have engaged a man and his wife and so far they suit me exactly, working men here expect plenty of meat and potatoes to every meal but I stick to my meal of porridge every morning. I find I can milk well, have milked four cows twice today. We steal half the milk from each cow and let the calves suck the rest. I ride to church in Emporia every Sunday morning, have dinner there, a chat with a friend and then back in time to feed etc. Soon the cattle will be out to grass and able to feed themselves but we shall be busy amongst the crops then. I keep in perfect health, have not had a headache or cold this winter. My farm is beautifully situated and has more natural advantages than any place I have seen. Plenty of timber too, but none close to the house which stands high. Marian sends me good accounts of the children, I do long for a peep at the little dears. We have plenty of little calves and pigs, and expect a foal daily; May and Jack would be delighted with them. I have no news.

Your affec. son,
John.

Emporia April 23 1885

Dear Mother,

We have at last got clear of winter and for the last month have had delightful weather, hardly any rain and quite warm. Grass is growing splendidly and the prairie is covered with beautiful flowers. I have been very busy the last ten days planting out a new orchard and vineyard, we have had some grand rain since I finished which makes them seem to grow. The soil here is wonderfully rich and grows everything to perfection provided it only gets enough rain. Gooseberries, plums and grapes grow wild about the place and all make nice preserves. All my stock has come through the winter wonderfully well and now they are out at grass you can almost see them grow. I wish you could only see the place I am sure you would like it. As soon as I can afford it I shall have a photo taken and will send you one. The river running through the farm has plenty of nice fish in it, some very large. Last summer the man living here caught one weighing 6 lbs. They all seem much better flavoured than English freshwater fish. I suppose these constant rumours of war cannot help keeping back any improvement in trade. From all the letters I get I have seen no cause to regret having come out here, I only wish I had taken the step earlier.

The other day I thought I would like some oxtail soup, my butcher said he always throws the tails away as no one wanted them. He saves them for me now and charges me nothing for them. Quite a lot of things we think a good deal of they either throw away or sell very cheap. All kinds of provisions are very cheap here especially if you buy them wholesale. A fat cow is only worth 3 cents a pound, still you cannot buy any meat under 10 or 12 cents. I am buying about twenty sheep so can kill one occasionally, they can be bought for 8 shillings each. I have six turkeys, four sitting now, so with lots of chickens with the exception of groceries shall have very little to buy.

Hoping you are feeling better,

Your affec. Son,

John.

Emporia August 17 1885

My dear Mother,

I wish you were near enough to pay me a visit and have a peep at my surroundings. I get plenty of fresh air and plenty of hard work and feel as well as possible. We had a wet spring and prospects for a good crop looked but slim, but lately all has gone splendidly. Corn I planted on June 25th is now 7 feet high, has grown at least two inches in height every day for the last 30 days. I could not believe vegetation could grow as quickly as it does in Kansas. Cattle are doing splendidly, everything in good health. We are living now almost entirely off the farm, have lots of milk, butter and chickens, bacon, eggs and tomatoes and sweetcorn and any amount of beautiful apples, so get along first class. I never enjoyed my food as I do here. We have breakfast at 6, dinner at 12, and supper at 6. I have just finished three weeks steady haymaking, have put up 12 large stacks so don't think either man or beast will starve this winter. Our place looks like a zoo; we have 90 hogs big and little, the place seems fairly alive with livestock: horses, cows, dogs, pigs, poultry, cats and turkeys in every direction. They give us lots of work one way and another, with so much stock some are sure to be in mischief. We had about a month hot weather both night and day perspiration rolling off us all the time, now days are warm but nights are cool and pleasant. My skin is in splendid order it has not troubled me a particle since I came out. I continue to have good reports from home. It will be 12 months since I left England by the time this reaches you. I would give a good deal to have a peep at you all. I have no news that would interest you. I was sorry to hear of Mr Shaw's death, he was a nice man.

Your affec. Son,

John.

The last sentence refers to the death of Mr Robert Shaw JP of Colne Hall (1809–1885), cotton manufacturer. His daughter, Elizabeth, was married to John's brother, Thomas Whitworth. He was also the grandfather of Helen Whitworth from whose stay in Kansas many letters follow below.

Emporia Oct 9 1885

My dear Father,

Thanks for your letter of Sept. 24th. The £100 will come in very useful and enable me to get through the winter without selling any stock as everything in the livestock line are very low just now. What the cause is I can hardly say but spring will most likely put a better face on things. I have a fine lot of cattle in splendid condition. My stock consists of 52 head of cattle, 17 horses and about 85 hogs. We have had only moderate crops, too much wet too early in the summer, in one 48 hours it rained 8 inches. We are now having perfect weather, cloudless skies and agreeable temperatures which will probably last till Christmas. All our crops will be safely harvested by the end of this week, then for a few months we shall only have our stock to feed and any little improvements we may need. The climate suits me exactly. I have not missed a working day since I started. We have two nice orchards and this spring I put out 200 more trees, I planted 120 vines which have made wonderful growth and will bear freely next summer so that with fruit, vegetables, eggs, milk and poultry we almost live on the products of the place with the exception of a little fresh meat and groceries. I find plenty to interest me and if I only had Marian and the children here should be as contented as possible. My bilious attacks are all gone and my skin is as clear as a bell and I sleep like a top. It will be slow making a fortune out of farming but my riches, like Brotherton's* will have to consist of the fewness of my wants. I do trust Business will soon look up and put you all in good spirits.

With best love to all at home,
Your affectionate son,
John.

* *Mr Joseph Brotherton was the first MP for Salford from 1832 until his death in 1857. On the pedestal of his statue in Peel Park, Salford are inscribed the words of Brotherton's motto 'My riches consist not in the extent of my possessions but in the fewness of my wants.'*

Emporia Dec 15 1885

My dear Mother,

I have not heard from any of you for some time. We have had a delightful Fall but the winter began with the second week in December ice three inches thick and plenty of snow. All we can do now is feed the animals. I think I told you my man's wife had a baby 9 weeks ago, she is still totally unfit for work so told them they would have to leave Jany. 1st. Since then they have acted like two spoiled children both as sulky as possible, the woman hasn't spoken a word to me since. I shall be delighted to see the last of them. I have paid her three months wages for doing nothing besides having the house upset and this is how they show their gratitude. I shall be glad when Marian gets out as this style of things is perfectly miserable. I have been having bad luck with my hogs: cholera has been raging round Emporia all summer and now has attacked mine, I have lost about 40 and may lose more. I am glad to have good accounts of Marian, she seems to be gaining strength nicely, children also seem flourishing. How disappointed Father must be with the Elections, I am perfectly ashamed of Manchester and Liverpool.* I see from the papers Father was defeated and by a pretty big majority too. I keep wonderfully well and hearty and if household matters were only more comfortable should get along very well. We have had clear skies and no rain for three months now; we have to haul water for hogs and horses. We get nearly all our rain in March, April, May and June. I have very little news as I have stuck close to the farm lately.

Your affec. Son,
John.

* *When the General Election came in late November it found Benjamin Whitworth deprived of his old constituency of Drogheda which, as a result of the Reform Bill, had become merged into the Co. Louth constituency. He looked elsewhere for another seat: he was first named as a candidate for Shoreditch, but finally decided to stand for Lewisham, Kent. The conservative Lord Lewisham defeated him at the poll by 4,244 votes to 3,019. After this election he gave up all ideas of a further parliamentary career. The Tories were victorious in all except one seat in Liverpool, and in all except one seat in Manchester.*

The following letter was published in the *Manchester Times* 3rd July 1886 under the heading

Farming in Kansas

The following letter has been received by the brother of a gentleman well known to everyone in the cotton trade, who went to America in 1884 and after inspecting most of Illinois (sic) and Kansas, bought 350 acres cultivated land, well fenced and watered, in the latter state. The letter gives his experience which may be of interest to anyone thinking of going out West with the intention of farming.'

Emporia, Kansas 9th June 1886

Dear Tom,

Your welcome letter duly to hand. We are now in the midst of our busiest season working hard from morning to night. Our crops are looking splendid, maize (or corn as it is called here) already some four feet high, and will soon be too tall to cultivate; unlike most crops it is planted in hills equal distances apart by an ingenious machine called a check rower, so that it can be cultivated in any direction, making as it were avenues of corn; the oftener it is stirred the better the crop. I have already cultivated mine twice each way and a prettier piece of corn I never saw, and with favourable weather it looks like 80 bushels an acre. It is a paying crop on a stock farm, as the stems and leaves when cut and put into shocks, are quite equal in feeding qualities to the quantity of prairie hay that could be grown in the same area, and when cut green, and the corn just beginning to harden, the hogs eat it up clean, stems and all, and fatten rapidly. I plucked an ear last year that weighed 1 1/2 lb and had 1,300 grains on it. Luckily farmers here don't know the virtue of manure, so was able to buy pure sheep manure straight from covered sheds dry as guano and nearly as rich, for 15 cents a load, as much as I could pile on the wagon and haul home, and its effect will last at least four years. The dark vivid green of my corn shows it is appreciated by the plants. I am also growing a good breadth of sugar cane, mostly used for molasses, but makes excellent sugar; sown thickly and cut early it makes excellent feed for cattle, and I can raise six tons an acre. I have also some millet. It grows finely here. My chief objection to farming here is the length of the winters, as one has to feed one's stock for at least five months. I am sowing tame grass as fast as possible. Blue grass, orchard grass and clover all grow splendidly and when my pasture gets seeded down to tame grasses it will lessen my feeding by six weeks at least since the natural grasses here are slow to come and quick to go. Stock very low in price here just now, cattle and hogs only worth 3 1/2 cents per lb live weight, but then their feed is proportionately cheap. I bought good hay last winter for 6s per ton; it is cut and stacked same day, no tending required. We mow it and rake it together and drag it to the stack with a machine made on the farm in two minutes and rejoicing in the name of 'Go Devil'. Two horses can collect it as fast as it can be stacked. Grass could have been bought standing in this neighbourhood for 50c an acre. Hogs pay better than any other stock here if only one can keep clear of the dreaded hog cholera, which, once it breaks out, seems to carry everything before it. I have 48 pigs from six sows having the run of the clover patch, and growing visibly, if all goes well should weigh 250 lbs each by Christmas. I don't intend to keep any hogs except for breeding stock over winter, as I find I can make pork in summer at a third of the price I can in winter. When English farmers find out clover will grow hogs quicker than corn they will make more money. The Poland China is the favourite breed here, and will compare favourably with the best English breeds, and with good keep will gain 1 1/2 lb a day in weight. Small fruits grow well here. Grapes I planted a year ago last spring have two or three bunches on apiece and have made wonderful growth. Apples grow splendidly, pears not so well. I like the climate first rate. About six weeks in winter far too cold and the same time in summer too warm, but the balance of the year as near perfection as could be wished for. Up to now (9 June) have worked in the fields all day with greatest ease. Living very cheap here. Steaks 10c a lb, but many parts we esteem highly can be bought very low. Ox tails the butcher will save for you and make no charge, and can get four or five pound flank pieces same cuts as they serve as pressed beef in the clubs for 2c per lb. – bacon and hams also equally cheap; but everyone feeds and kills their own. With the exception of a little fresh meat and groceries, I need buy nothing eatable, as I have plenty of milk, butter, eggs, chickens, turkeys, vegetables and a great variety of fruit. Tomatoes, cucumbers and water melons grow in profusion. I have now been here two years and continue to like the country: the continual outside life suits my health and I have not had any serious ailment during the whole time I have been here, and have gained fully a stone in weight. The only drawback is being without my family, but hope soon to have them come out with me, in which case I should be perfectly content to settle down here for good. I work along with my men and take my fair share doing as much as any of them, and finish up the day with a swim in the river that runs through my farm. I have never regretted leaving the cotton trade, and though not making one's fortune in farming, yet live comfortably and without anxiety which is something to be thankful for.

Emporia Dec 16 1886

My dear Mother,

I am sorry to hear both from Ben and Marian you had been ill again, I hope by the time this reaches you you will be quite well again, it will perhaps reach you in time to wish you a Happy New Year. I am quite well again after my sick spell. I only weighed 138 lbs, last week when in town I weighed myself again and found I was 156 lbs, my usual weight, a pretty good gain to make in a month. Nothing has so far been definitely settled about my coming over but I hope to do so shortly. I must be back by early March anyhow. We have had one or two cold spells already, one night we had 42 degrees of frost.* Since then we have had several bright English June days. We have had very little rain for the last twelve months not more certainly than you often have in one week in England. Nicholai** is a great help to me and a nice companion, he is very anxious to make himself useful and seems to like being here very much indeed. We have had no housekeeper for three months and have managed first rate. I am the chief cook and Nick says a very good one. I have 37 fine turkeys, I wish I could have sent you one for Christmas. They are only worth 4d lb ready for eating. I have pretty good accounts from home; May and Jack write me every week, they are evidently getting along first rate at school.*** Jack, they tell me, reads quite well, neither of them knew a letter when I left home. Baby will have altered the most, I am sure I would not recognise her if I met her in the street. Business seems to be improving a little, I hope it will continue to do so.

With fondest love to all at home,
Your affec. Son,
John.

---

* The winter of 1886/7 turned out to be extremely severe: 'on the ninth day of January a north wind spewed out an inch of snow an hour; the storm continued for ten days. By January 15 the thermometer was forty-six below zero, and the world was white. On January 28, the Great Blizzard struck again. For seventy two hours, it seemed as if all the world's ice from time's beginnings had come on a wind that howled and screamed with the fury of demons. It was a tornado of white frozen dust. When the storm ended, millions of open-range cattle were scattered for miles, dead or dying ... the gulches and coulees were filled with snow to depths of a hundred feet or more levelling the land. Ranch houses were completely drifted over.' (Dee Brown 1995 The American West, p. 331)

** Nicholai Martyn Whitworth was John Whitworth's first cousin once removed. He was the eldest son of 'old Nicholai' Whitworth and his wife

Martha ('Polly') Stone. His father, 'old Nicholai', had been born at Nicholiev in Russia on 31 October 1844 when his father, William Whitworth, was building lighthouses on the Caspian and Black Sea coasts. Later William Whitworth settled in Drogheda as the resident partner of Benjamin Whitworth and Brothers. 'Old Nicholai' also lived in Drogheda, in Paradise Square, and succeeded his father as managing director of the cotton mills at Greenmount, Drogheda. Nicholai Martyn Whitworth was brought up in Drogheda. (See the Whitworth family tree.)

*** May and Jack Whitworth attended a school run by Miss Morris and Miss Croft in Bowdon.

New York March 26th 1887 R.M.S. '*Republic*'

My dear Mother,

We have had a roughish trip, heavy seas nearly all the time, but Marian, Nurse and the children have stood it splendidly. They were all sick a little but nothing to speak of. The people on board made a great fuss of the children, they have enjoyed themselves wonderfully. The Captain took a great fancy to Daisy and Walter. He got the Steward to make them toffee. They all look wonderfully well. I caught cold first day out and have felt pretty seedy all the way. We saw lots of whales and one day passed quite a number of icebergs, two quite large ones, so the children will have something to remember. We have only 26 cabin passengers but over 1,000 steerage, mostly German and Irish. Marian looks better for the trip.

We have not been able to be very much on deck as she has pitched and rolled too much to be pleasant. We had to change tickets at the last moment, the '*Celtic*', the one we ought to have come by having sustained considerable injury in a storm coming home. The '*Republic*' is a nice boat, we have nothing to complain about. Marian sends her love to you all.

Your affec. Son,
John.

The Port of New York, Ship's Manifest for the R.M.S. '*Republic*' arrived 26th March 1887 from Liverpool and Queenstown. Peter John Irving, Master, records the following:

1st Cabin Class
Cabin 16:

Jno Whitworth	age 43	farmer
Mrs Whitworth	age 37	wife
Miss Mary Whitworth	age 8	child
Miss Daisy Whitworth	age 6	child
Master Jno Whitworth	age 4	child
Master Walter Whitworth	age 3	child
Infant	infant	
A. Simpson	age 18	nurse

In the **2nd Cabin Class** list was:

W. H. Falconer age 30   salesman of Manchester, England.

The **Summary of Passengers** on this voyage shows:

Steerage	2nd Cabin Class	1st Cabin Class
27 US citizens	3 US citizens	5 US citizens
200 English	18 English	21 English
189 Irish	3 Irish	2 Canadians
170 Swedes	1 Scotch	28 Total
44 Norwegians	25 Total	
22 Russians		
6 Italians		
35 Germans		
693 Total		

The family's first impression of America must have been very similar to that described in 1891 by Richard Lovett in his book *United States Pictures* (which has recently been re-issued as *America 100 years ago, The Beauty of Old America illustrated*). He describes the approach to New York by sea as follows:

The eye that for six or seven days has had to content itself with the somewhat limited range of colours afforded by the blue and gray and white of the Atlantic in calm and storm, and the wider though limited range of colouring afforded by the ocean sky, feasts with delight upon the soft hues of the New Jersey hills, and upon the lovely islets and wooded slopes of New York harbour. The great steamer slowly and with dignity makes her way along the winding channel and through the Narrows, amid the fleet of varied shipping, and past the lofty Statue of Liberty until at length the commercial capital of the Republic lies before her. The statue had been unveiled by President Cleveland on 28th October 1886. On its base is inscribed The New Colossus, a poem by Emma Lazarus written in 1883:

'Not like the brazen giant of Greek fame
With conquering limbs astride from land to land,
Here at our sea-washed, sunset gates shall stand
A mighty woman with a torch, whose flame
Is the imprisoned lightning, and her name
Mother of Exiles - from her beacon hand
Glows world-wide welcome; her mild eyes command
The air-bridged harbor that twin cities frame.
'Keep, ancient lands, your storied pomp!' cries she
With silent lips 'Give me your tired, your poor,
Your huddled masses yearning to breathe free
The wretched refuse of your teeming shores,
Send these, the homeless, tempest-tost to me
I lift my lamp beside the golden door!'

'On every side signs of life and industry abound. Saucy little tugs puff noisily about the lovely bay. Scores and scores of vessels, from the great ocean liner down to the tiny sloop, crowd the wide waterways. Numerous lines of large steam ferry boats cross the river and the harbour in every direction and as a newcomer looks with eager interest upon the city he is at once impressed by three things: the dense masses of shipping that crowd the wharves, the enormous piles of buildings that uprear themselves into the sky, as though bent upon realising the never completed purpose of the builders of the original Tower of Babel, and the great bridge so skillfully thrown across the broad East River at such a height that the masts of the largest vessels pass easily beneath it.

'There are no docks of the kind so common at Liverpool and London. All the shipping from small barges up to the steamer of 10,000 tons, discharges and takes on board cargo and passengers from wharves that jut out into the Hudson and East Rivers. And no sooner has the great vessel been safely moored to the wharf than the great ordeal of the Customs House has to be encountered. So far as consumption of time goes, the writer's experience is that the Customs House at New York is less troublesome than at Liverpool. But since in England the list of dutiable articles contains about twelve items which in the United States is about twelve hundred, the search at New York is

not infrequently an exasperating and troublesome experience. Until the Inspector has chalked certain hieroglyphics upon each article of baggage, the traveller must bear this infliction as best he can; but as soon as this is done he is at liberty to take himself and his belongings whithersoever he desires ...

'The great steamship companies land their passengers in the immediate neighbourhood of the Cunard Company Pier No 39 North River, as the Hudson is commonly called near its mouth, or on the Jersey shore opposite.' Before proceeding further it was necessary for newly arrived immigrants to pass through the official Emigrant Landing Depot at Castle Garden, near the Battery at the tip of Manhattan. 'Inside the huge rotunda - an area of 50,000 square feet, capable of holding between 2,000 and 4,000 people - the immigrant could obtain food and information, collect letters, change money, book accommodation at a boarding house, buy rail and steamboat tickets, and arrange for his luggage to be forwarded... It made it possible a more orderly and systematic handling of passengers and their luggage, for only licensed runners and agents were allowed to enter... . the whole enterprise was financed by a head tax on immigrants which ranged from one to two dollars and which Captains usually added to the fare...

'Throughout the 1880s there were repeated complaints about the way it was being run. It was alleged that employees were given to bullying and that railroad agents and money changers licensed to operate there were defrauding immigrants on an extensive scale...' (M.A.Jones 1976 p. 45f).

The Whitworth family travelled on westwards from New York by train. The American railway carriages had better windows than those in England - and if one travelled in a luxurious Wagner Palace Car one could see the views through the large plate glass windows from the comfort of an armchair. The average speed was slower than on British trains but it made the journey more comfortable and easier to move about the carriage and use the observation platforms. There was a marked absence of bridges and fences and a high number of level crossings which necessitated the constant use of the hoarse steam whistle. The stations were rather utilitarian: platforms were almost unknown, and there were few waiting rooms or other conveniences. Long-distance trains were often an hour or two late. Travelling by train across the Great plains in the 1890s was described by Lovett:

'The impression produced is exactly that of being at sea, only instead of ploughing one's way through the yielding and shifting water, one skims the surface of the solid but level land. Signs of population occur in

the constant succession of little farmsteads which dot the landscape here and there. Almost all of them painted white, sometimes a red or chocolate colour, and nearly everyone is provided with a small windmill for the purpose of pumping water. In this way the breezes, which constantly sweep the prairie are turned to a very practical use... Everywhere a country in the process of being settled passes under the eye. This effect is heightened every now and then by the sight of a "prairie schooner" that is an emigrant party crossing the prairie in wagons, carrying with them their family and possessions, and taking several weeks to make the journey accomplished by the luxurious train in twenty-four hours.'

Emporia April 24th 1887

My dear Mother,

We have got pretty well settled down in our new home but we have not yet begun to alter the house. We find it rather crowded but they all seem to like it much better than staying at the hotel in Emporia. We are all as busy as bees from morning to night, the children are all wild with delight at the different animals about the place. They ask the most curious questions about everything. May and Jack's great occupation at present is finding eggs and feeding the chickens, taking the cows to water and lots of odd jobs. Daisy peels potatoes splendidly. They all look first rate, really healthy and bonny, and one and all have famous appetites. Jack begins to ride nicely, he rode a horse all by himself today. Marian had a bad cold when she first arrived, indeed we all had, caused by the railway cars being so abominably overheated. Now she looks better than I have seen her in a long time. We got Helena's letter when we were in town today and were glad to hear you were all well. We put three seats into one of our farm wagons and take the whole lot into church, Marian and I, Emma, Nicholai, and Mr Faulkner.* The children were much excited, everything is so fresh and new for them. Baby toddles about the place for hours chasing the little pigs and chickens. Farming shows distinct signs of improvement: land has risen, hogs which were only 3/4 cents when I left now worth 5 cents. May told Marian the other day she was going to make some poetry, she only got two lines which were as follows

This poem is mine

How thy sweet lineaments do shine

Last Sunday Marian told Daisy to go to bed, instead of asking Emma** to undress her she got into bed just as she was, boots and all, and we only found it out next morning. She seemed to think she had done a wonderfully clever thing.

With love to all,

Your affec. Son,

John

* *Walter H. Falconer (sometimes spelt Faulkner in the letters) was born on 11th July 1857 in Manchester, England. He travelled out to Emporia with John Whitworth and his family in March 1887, in order to help on the Whitworth farm; he had previously been a salesman in Manchester.*

** *Emma was the nursemaid brought out from England, whose proper name was Amy Simpson.*

On his return from England John Whitworth did not waste much time in purchasing additional land for his farm. He purchased the northwest quarter of the northeast quarter of Section 8 Township 19 south Range 12 from H.C. Whitley and Katie Whitley (husband and wife) for $500, on 4th April 1887.

**THE LETTERS
PART II**

Summer 1887

THE EMPORIA DAILY REPUBLICAN Thursday 5th May 1887 (page 1)

John Whitworth, who resided four miles east of this city had his house totally destroyed by fire on Monday 2nd inst. Mr Whitworth purchased the place about one year ago (sic) and had just returned from England with his family, bringing with him a large outfit of household furnishings and goods which were consumed by the flames. His wife lost a gold watch valued at seven hundred dollars. Mr Whitworth lost his gold watch and about eighty dollars in money. Valuable carpets, clothing and furniture, and many things highly prized by the family which cannot be replaced, were also consumed. The total loss was about $8,000.00. The house was partially insured. Through the efforts of neighbours his barn and some other property was saved. Our informant, D.M. May, says that Mr Whitworth intends to rebuild as soon as possible. He occupies a small tenant house on the place for the time being.'

Bowdon, Emporia, Kansas, 3rd May 1887
(Marian to her eldest brother, Abraham Haworth)

My dear Brother,
    I have written a letter to Mother as nearly as I can remember like one I wrote last night, when I little thought the sad fate it and many other things would have to share before the sun went down again. I thought I would write you all particulars and you would tell Mother in the way you thought best. The girl I brought out with me is a very clean and respectable girl, but like most of her class self-willed and quite persuaded she could never do any harm. Both John and I have been constantly warning and cautioning her against fire, she would throw hot ashes outside. Mrs Smith, our kind neighbour I told Mother about, was not well enough to come and help to wash. Emma did not like her way of washing, just with very little water. There are no real wash boilers here. There are large pans they put on the stove to boil the clothes. We have a new fine boiler for pigs, with a place for a fire underneath, Emma got hold of this with great triumph. I thought she was only going to use it for keeping a reserve of water for rinsing etc. I left her entirely to attend to the house. We were just finishing dinner when John saw a great cloud of smoke behind the house and all ran out and met Emma looking so frightened who said the ice-house was on fire. The ice-house is two or three yards behind the woodshed, the woodshed is connected to the house, and is right against both kitchens. It was useless to do anything with the ice-house. We did all we could to keep it from the woodshed by deluging the woodshed with water, but we had not much water. We had two barrels of water on a wagon. John drew the wagon up to the woodshed and

poured water on as hard as possible. We also kept Emma at the pump, but in spite of all our efforts a great tongue of flame seemed to blow over the roof of the shed. John cried out 'All of you get out of the house, the house is gone'. He said 'Where is baby?' I was so dazed I could not think where she was so I ran out of one room into another until I came to the bedroom where I had put her for her mid-day sleep. I carried her out and got the children round me, and it was no use trying to go back into the house, because all the children would crowd round and follow me. John and the others were so spent in fighting the fire, but they rushed into the front of the house, and saved all the pictures, and the greater part of the books and a great part of the childrens' and my clothes, also all of the bedclothes and two mattresses. There was a large clothes closet in our bedroom where all John's clothes were, also some of my dresses, including my black satin and my next best dress, a silk mantle, a velvet jacket; frocks of Daisy's and May's, all the carpets we brought with us, books, shoes and everything belonging to John. John, after saving the pictures, rushed upstairs, and brought an armful of things, while he was in the room the fire broke through the landing window and he had the greatest difficulty in groping his way downstairs, suffocated with smoke, he said another gulp and he must have dropped. The front door was open, he could not see any door but at the last gasp found himself outside. Mr Falconer jumped through his bedroom window and landed on the ground unhurt. From the time of our first seeing the fire to the whole place being a heap of ruins was not more than 20 minutes. Our neighbours came to our assistance with astonishing rapidity in less than quarter of an hour I counted 12 horses hitched up in different places, and only one with a saddle on, but only 3 were in time to save anything from the house. The chimney stacks stayed up to the last, they swayed to and fro in the wind, it was uncertain which way they would fall. There was a strong N.W. wind. About 35 yards to the E of the house there is a large stone stable and barn, the basement is stone, the barn part is frame. The original contract for building was $1,200. John had also spent some money on it, it is considered by far the best in this part of the county. It seems nothing short of a miracle how the barn was saved. Mr Smith, the husband of Mrs Smith I have written about, is a strong powerful man 6ft 2 or 3 inches, he was a soldier the whole of the Civil War, he was determined to fight for the barn to the last. Everyone felt what a forlorn hope it was, but he stationed men on the roof. There is a well on one side of the barn and a pump at the other where the windmill is: they hauled buckets by the windmill pulleys. They let out all the animals from the stables. Men were at the doors, as the great pieces of burning embers came floating on the place, the men and boys on the roof poured water, and the men at the bottom of the building beat the fire out with spades, the whole place was wreathed in smoke, and for nearly half an hour the fight seemed hopeless, but every man and boy worked like a hero. As I stood watching I could only pray that no one might be hurt or injured, I felt I did not care if every stitch and stick perished, if everyone was saved. This was granted. Our man had one side of his hair and whiskers singed off, one I know had his hands cut, and many were blistered. I counted 28 men and boys after the fire, and then there were our 3. It is marvellous that no one was hurt, you would have been more struck with this if you could have seen the mad, furious way the wind shot out the great tongues of flame.

I am staying with 3 of the children at Mrs Smith's, the other children and the nurse are at another neighbours, but I must not keep them up. Mr Smith and Mr May are staying up with our menkind to watch the smouldering embers are not fanned into a flame by the wind.

<u>Wednesday morning</u> This morning is just as perfect and lovely as it is possible to imagine, blue skies, trees in their lovely spring dress, the birds with bright plumage and song making the scene of desolation more marked by contrast. Our loss is very great, and yet are like the changes that come in the wheel of fortune, our mercies are greater than our losses. 'He stayeth His rough wind in the day of His East wind'. It has brought all the kindliness and goodness of our neighbours out in a way nothing else would. Three of the men who helped with the fire owed John money. They came up after the fire and said they would see he had his money back as soon as they could get it. One man rode off and brought back all he possessed, another elderly man came over this morning to offer his son's services with ploughing to work off his debt of $15. John had bought several lots of corn from a farmer who said he could not let him have any more, he should want it all for himself, he said to John 'You need not trouble paying me for that corn, it will do anytime next year, and you can have as much more as you want.' Mr May, the Quaker neighbour, when the fire was over and John was pacing round, stood by his side, and followed him about in mute sympathy. It was beyond words. He and his wife offered to take us all in, if we could put up with their rough ways. My gold watch and chain and also John's and $100.00 of paper notes between us (were lost). I went into the room to look for baby, and yet never thought to bring anything away. I must have had my hand on where they lay and yet never thought to bring anything away. It was only this morning when John said his watch was gone that I remembered I had a watch at all.

There seems a strange irony about the things that were saved. There was a dressing table with a mirror I had a particular objection to, and was quite determined to scrap it. Two men risked their lives to save this. Our beautiful bedroom suite of walnut as well as all their contents have perished. There is an old lamp broken with the base fixed in a preserve jar, only used to go in the back kitchen with, this is carefully preserved. John had a pair of corduroy trousers which a cow had horned and ripped from top to bottom, these with a thick Melton hunting coat, a summer pair of trousers, two pairs of hunting breeches and a dress coat form his entire wardrobe. From a very extensive stock he has fared worse than anyone. He saved his guns, pistols and fishing rods. A beautiful fishing rod he threw out on the lawn was burnt up just from the heat of the fire. We have saved 7 of the very largest cases we took out with us, a few chairs, a bookcase and a table. I don't know what we shall do. John wants me and the children to go back into town, this I am very unwilling to do for many reasons, for one thing we should require more than all the money we have in the bank to pay for us there for the next month. Another thing it would be most miserable for John and the other two to eat and sleep in the barn. I don't care for the man's wife, she is a dirty, grasping, selfish woman. I would not like them to be dependent upon her tender mercies. There are two cottages on the place: one of them would make a good dining room and kitchen, the other would have three rooms which Emma, myself and the children could sleep in. I think we should get them fixed up. John and the other two can sleep in the barn until the house is built. Nothing will persuade me to have another frame house built. I have the greatest dread of them, since Mrs Crossley told me about the fate of her brother's house last summer, which was identical almost with ours in all its details. Ours was set on fire from washing, theirs from cooking. The house was insured for $1,500.00, the barn for $1,000.00. The man, Charlie, went to inform the Insurance Company of the fire as soon as the fire was over, and brought back letters, one of them from Walter and one from Lily. I will answer both, all being well, in a few days. We had insured all we brought with us while it was on the sea and on the railroads, and had intended to insure the furniture and clothes, but had not had the opportunity to do so. Poor John, he is so down, he had been so light-hearted, full of hope and courage, and seemed bubbling over with joy, more like a schoolboy, now he had the children and me with him. It is a sad blow, and yet it might have been much worse had any life been lost, had the barn gone, the cow stables, sheds and hay pens and windmill must inevitably have gone too. They are only a few yards East and considering there was not 16 minutes to get the things out and only 3 hired men to do it – the 3 outsiders were not there more than 3 or 4 minutes, it is more than wonderful how much was saved. 3 wagons and the weighing machine for livestock were the only outside things that

Marian's mother, Marianne Haworth née *Jones, widow of Smallshaw Lomax Haworth.*

were burnt. The men broke down the fences to stop the fire from spreading. Our house was always spoken of as 'the Big House across the river' and was considered a very fine place. John says he has never seen or heard of a fire the 2 ½ years he has been here. While he was away in England our next neighbour to the south was burnt out. He is building up now. He said he could sympathise with us more than anyone. I had been congratulating myself on my packing. It is wonderful how the china and ornaments had come without a chip. The drawing room clock and set, the carriage clock, two black Wedgewood bowls, salad bowl, part of my best china tea service alone remains out of two large skips that came from you. I found the skips carried things with perfect safety; they gave and swayed whilst the cases vibrated. I had a dinner service in a case, the travelling made sad havoc with them. From the fire and perils by land and sea out of 197 pieces I have 18 plates saved. You must not worry about me, though I cannot help feeling grieved about things, which no amount of money could give back their associations, yet above and beyond everything is the feeling of thankfulness for all the precious life saved. Poor Emma, her life long she will have to carry remorse for her

*Marian's brothers, Abraham, Jesse and Walter Haworth,
and her sister Harriet*

carelessness. The bitter part is that it was such criminal carelessness. Anyone with the least observation of the dryness and the way the wind blows here would never have lighted a fire outside except in a cleared place, and far enough from any wood. She is so heartbroken I cannot say anything to her. She told Mrs Woodson she had tried 4 times to come to America, and now she had come, she had been the means of bringing so much trouble. She wished she had never come and was now at the other side of the world. It is a life experience for her, but dearly bought at our expense. Had the fire broken out when the men were in the fields, nothing could have been saved, or had we altered the house and unpacked all our things it would have been far worse. They think it will be about a month before we receive our insurance money. By the time we hear from you we will perhaps be forgetting about the past, and looking forward with plans and hopes for another start. I have only been here little more than a fortnight in which there has been a prairie fire and our house demolished by the same force: fire is a cruel, fearful thing, more like demons let loose than anything else. Give my love to everybody and ask them not to worry, I should be more grieved than anything to know that our troubles are causing others trouble.

I am always your affectionate sister,
Marian.

Emporia May 10 1887
(John to his mother, Jane Whitworth)

My dear Mother,
We have had a great misfortune since I last wrote. Our new girl proved very careless with fire. I spoke to her again and again about it. Last Monday she set the house on fire, we all tried to put it out but being very short of water we could do nothing. It all burnt to the ground in 15 minutes. Luckily we were all at dinner at the time and managed to save a good many things, but they are chiefly the childrens'. I have not got a coat to put on and only the boots I am wearing. I lost the gold watch father gave me and Marian lost her gold one also. I managed to save all the pictures and a good many other things but a great many are gone. We were sure the barn would go also but many neighbours came to help us and we saved it, although it caught fire several times. I had a small house on the place which I got moved up and we have very comfortable quarters considering. Nick, myself and Mr Falconer sleep in the barn and the rest in the house. We had the house insured and intend rebuilding it in stone next time. It keeps very dry here, only one shower since we came. Crops

John Whitworth's sisters: Mary with her husband
James Boyd; Helena and Bessie

suffering considerably, wells played out. We have to go two miles for drinking water, we have had no severe rain for eighteen months. Marian and the children all look first rate. I cannot write more as we have only one pen.

Your affec. Son,
John.

Emporia, Kansas 10 May 1887
(Marian to her elder brother, Jesse Haworth)

My dear Jesse,
Many thanks for yours written from Matlock. I hope you are feeling the usual benefits from your stay there. You would miss Sergeant Montgomery. I should think it would be very difficult to fill his place. How very interesting it was to meet Mr and Mrs Whistler, personally I should like to thank him for *The Lady of the Woods*. It is something to be able to carry it in one's mind's eye, such a picture of loveliness. I can often see it in all its beauty with my eyes shut. You would hear of our sad misfortune in having our house burnt to the ground. It is most aggravating because it was so preventable. The girl I bought out with us suits me very well indeed. She is very kind to the children, clean, respectable and good principled, but she could not be made to see how careless she was about fire .... I had the greatest dread in coming to live in a frame house because of fire. It seems strange to think how soon my presentiment should be realised, but I did not think I should pass through the ordeal as well as I have done. It was a terrible thing, one half hour to be sitting at dinner, the next everything to be a mass of ruins. It is wonderful how much was saved considering there was not more than 5 minutes to save. At first we fought the fire, now we see it would have been better just to have used all our energies in getting things out of the house because every second was of moment. The season has been so dry the house was like so much kindlewood. If we could have had all the help we had after the first ten minutes, at the very first, all would have been saved, but ..... our nearest neighbours are half a mile away.

When I feel inclined to grieve as I recollect one thing after another of which not the slightest trace remains, I just recall how near John was to loosing his life – and how many lives were in peril, and all came out unharmed, then I can only be thankful. The house was considered a very large one in these parts and was always spoken of as the big house. It certainly was very pretty, but to me with such standards as Woodside, Hilston House and Ecclesfield and others, it was a very modest place. But we were beginning to make it into a very homelike place..........On Sunday

I had thought as I looked at our dinner table, set out with flowers and our silver freshly cleaned, if our friends at home could see us they would be very satisfied, and if we had them near us and our house a little larger and more convenient we should have nothing more to wish for. The next day the scene was changed entirely – such is life. Mr Ingalls* heard of the fire and came over at once. He was very kind, he said he thought it was the prettiest place he had seen in Kansas. It is indeed a lovely spot, and that remains to us. John has two cottages on this place, we are utilising these and are under the circumstances, very comfortable indeed. A gentleman from Emporia, whose wife and family are out of town for a month, most kindly offered us the use of their house until their return, free gratis. I much prefer being near John – poor fellow he feels it more for my sake than his own. The children, I think enjoy the excitement of having had a fire, and think it rather grand than otherwise. They are particularly well. We have all been since we came out to the farm. There is an epidemic of measles in the neighbourhood, I hope we keep clear of it.

By the time you receive this all the excitement of the opening of the Exhibition and the Royal visit** will be a thing of the past. We are looking forward to the next paper with a full account of it all.

I suppose Marianne*** is as busy as ever. Give her my best love and accept much from your ever affectionate sister, Marian Whitworth.

The adjuster from the Insurance Company has not yet been out. We hope to build our next house of stone. There is plenty on the place – blue and also a reddish grey sandstone.

Dr Frank J. Ingalls was the pastor of the first Congregational Church at the intersection of 8th Avenue and Mechanics St., Emporia, and he was a good friend of John Whitworth. He was a native of Haverhill, Massachusetts and a graduate of Williams College. He began his ministry in the Congregational Church at Olathe, Kansas in 1870, where he was ordained. In 1872 he moved to Achison and during this time he took a year off to travel in Europe, Egypt, and the Holy Land. In 1884 he came to Emporia and was there for three years before being called to become President of Drury College. He died suddenly after a serious illness on 5th August 1892, aged about fifty. He was unmarried. He was a man of fine judgement, always firm and always for peace. He was a charming companion and his speech sparkled with gentle humour and apt expression.

**The Jubilee Exhibition which was visited by nearly five million visitors.*

***Jesse's wife, née Marianne Armitage.*

Emporia, Kansas 16th May 1887
(Marian to her mother-in-law, Jane Whitworth)

My dear Mother,
I intended writing to Mr Whitworth in time for his birthday: will you tell him with our love, we shall think and speak of him and wish him many happy returns when the day comes, and the children, all being well, will have a fete day. I hope you are not distressing yourself about our fire. Although it was undoubtedly a very great misfortune, we are not allowing ourselves to be at all cast down. Often in spite of myself I recall thing after thing that has perished and if I am in the least inclined to lament I remember how nearly John lost his life, then everything gives way to thankfulness.

They have no proper washing boilers in this part of the world, and to make matters worse the water is fearfully hard. London water is as soft as milk by comparison. They have large copper pans, like a large fish pan, which they put on the stove. They are dreadfully chary of water – they will pass a whole wash through the same water. Mrs. Smith, a neighbour, had helped us with our wash previously but this unfortunate day was too ill to come and did not seem to us that she would be well for some little time. Emma said she would do the wash herself and she was not going to be bothered by having the clothes washed in dirty water, she was going to have plenty. There were two heaters outside, I should call them boilers. We used them for water, there was, what I did not know, a place underneath for fire. I was busy in the house – she washed in the back kitchen, and had the copper as usual on the kitchen stove with clothes. Just as we finished dinner there was a great cloud of smoke from the back of the house, we all rushed out without hats, children as well, and found the house in flames. The Ice house was about two yards to the rear of the woodshed. The woodshed ran the length of the two kitchens and was connected to the house. It was something like this

*Plan of the original farm showing the icehouse,
woodshed and kitchens where the fire started*

... We fought the fire with all our might using every available drop of liquid. I emptied the milk out of the bowls, the boiling water out of the kettle and boilers and Mr Falconer emptied the swills on to the fire. There was a barrel of water on a wagon and John managed to draw the wagon close to the shed, but the fire licked the water up and consumed the wagon and the shed. John saw the shed was gone and the flames leaping up the house called 'Everyone to get out of the house, the house has gone.'....... We think a spark from the wretched heater must have blown into the Ice house and set some hay that was there on fire, because when we first saw it, the fire seemed to come from inside, but from the commencement to the whole being a heap of ruins was no more than half an hour. The house, though very well built, with the weather being so dry was just like so much kindlewood. I daresay we spent more than 10 minutes fighting the fire..... John has come off very badly in the matter of clothes. All his things were in a large clothes closet, which went out of our bedroom, they have them here instead of a dressing room. It was 3 times the size of our dressingroom at Glebelands and had hooks all round. I found it most convenient and I had arranged all John's clothes, at one end was a row of shelves where I had put all the carpets we brought out, and my best dresses, and many of the childrens' clothes. It was in trying to get some things out of this that he was in such great danger. While he was in this room the fire broke through the landing window, he could not see his way, and was almost choked with the heat and smoke, he groped with his hand on the bannister..... the front door was open and he was led out. Mr Falconer was trying to save his things, his bedroom door was on the other side of the landing to ours. He dare not face the clouds of smoke which met him when he opened his door, so he jumped through his bedroom window – a marvel how he escaped unhurt. Only two of our neighbours were in time to help us with our house.... In less than 20 minutes we had 28 men and boys – many of them just throwing themselves on their horses and riding bare-back and others running as they never ran before. There was a very strong wind blowing and, had it not been for the splendid way these good friends worked, our barn, stables and outbuildings must have gone as well as the farm implements..... The wind blew to them, the straw inside the barn was on fire several times. Men were on the roof knocking out, pouring water on great pieces of burning matter which flew about in the air. I shall never forget the awful cruelty, when the house was one solid glow and the great tongues of flame rising up it seemed into the sky and the people trying to save things. I felt if only they were out of the way and safe I should not care if every stitch and stick I had in the world went, if everyone escaped unhurt. As I stood with the children on the

side of the hill I could only pray that everyone might be safe. The more I
think of it the greater I see what a mercy it was no life was lost. We shall
soon get over the loss of our goods, though some things have gone
which money could not have bought me - yet if any lives had been lost,
say for instance Baby in bed – our whole lives would have been
saddened and we could hardly have bourne to look on or think of the
place. People have been so kind, instead of feeling in a strange land we
feel among friends. Mr. Ingalls has been so kind, he has twice been to
see us with some ladies from the congregation. One of them told me Mr.
Ingalls had said we had true English grit and pluck and I was as brave as
brave could be..... We are having true Western life in a shanty. I can tell
you a very good one. None of your ten-roomed places. We have a
diningroom 24 x 18ft, two good bedrooms, and the barn, which we call
the Hall, where the menkind sleep. It honestly is as comfortable as a
cottage at the seaside or in the country would be. We have bought all
household requisites eked out by a few things from the fire. We have a
gasoline stove which is a very wonderful summer arrangement; much
better than an English gas stove but perhaps not so safe. If we get the
insurance on the house all right we shall build our next house of stone as
there is plenty on the place. Our house was considered quite a palace by
our immediate neighbours, and was always spoken of as 'the big house
across the river.' My standard was larger than those who are accustomed
to call a shanty a home. We were making fun and joking on Sunday, the
day before the fire. I had worked very hard the week before to get the
house to my liking. I had had spring cleaning and the carpet up in John's
sitting room, I went to town and bought a lovely bookcase. John already
had a good one, and I also got a secretary: these went after 3 days
possession with their contents. I arranged the pictures three deep round
the room, I also had placed my china and nick nacks about the room. It
really was so pretty. At dinner we had flowers on the table and brightly
cleaned silver. Our bill of fare was roast Turkey, 3 vegetables and
Cabinet Pudding,* custard, tarts and 2 or 3 kinds of stewed fruit. With
the exception of flour and sugar all were raised on the place. I should
have been glad to see my grandest friends. We were laughing and saying
we how comfortable we were, and we said we would write a book called
The Hardships of a Western Ranch. In spite of the fire I do not regret
coming here. I feel attached to this place and the contretemps has roused
my mettle. I feel we must go through all difficulties, I could not run
away now. The children are very well and so am I. The chicks quite
enjoy the pic-nic life. The weather has been lovely though sometimes
too warm for my taste. Thank Helena for her letter with my love. I am
sorry Mary is not well, I trust by this she is better. Would you mind

sending her this letter as I have not time just at present to write another long letter. I will write to her in answer to her kind one as soon as I can. I want to get the house as comfortable as possible for the summer. I shall have to go through all my things to see where they can be put and what is likely to be wanted soon. You said you would answer every one of my letters, you now owe me two, don't forget.

With much love to all at Daleham Gardens,

I am always, dear Mother, your affectionate daughter,

M. Whitworth.

Cabinet Pudding is made from bread, egg custard and stoned raisins steamed in a pudding basin (see recipe in Mrs Beeton's Cookery and Household Management).

Bowdon, Emporia 19th June 1887
(Marian to her sister-in-law, Marianne Haworth)

My very dear Marianne,

Thank you so much for your letter which is the only one I have received from the Bowdon Circle for nearly a fortnight. I am so glad to hear that Mr Armitage* was able to get a view of the Exhibition. If you had the same weather we are having he would be able to live here if he wanted. I find the days very hot – if it were possible to lie on a couch reading all day with someone to fan the flies off, it would be delightful, and work in the early morning and evenings which are delightfully cool. The evenings are perfect. Both John and Mr. Ingalls say they remind them of Egypt, and certainly they remind me of Holman Hunt's pictures – the sky such a high expanse. The after glow tonight remained for more than two hours after sunset. We have made a good start with our new house. Men are at work getting out the old foundations and cellars. We expect the stonemasons will be able to get to work the week after next. I am afraid I shall not be able to give you a complete idea of our losses and salvage from the fire. There was a large skip and 3 other cases in the woodshed – these with all their contents were the first to go. I cannot remember all that was in them. I know that more than half our copies of Dickens and a great many other books, chiefly presents, and a valuable set of etchings of Turner's – not of course Liba Studio, but they were good and we hoped to have a good many of them framed. We had intended doing so for several years. My silver box with large stores of plated silver accumulated by Mrs Whitworth went in one of them. I was offered £18 by the second-hand dealer in books on the Downs for the complete set of Dickens. All our carpets except one were burnt. I am especially sorry to lose some persian rugs given to John by Mr Besso. Excepting the 4 cases in the woodshed and two in the barn I had unpacked everything. Our case in the barn contained my two sewing machines, a hand and a treadle. The other had our pretty brass clock and ornaments out of the Drawing Room, which you and Jesse gave us, and a good carpet and the remainder of our Dickens. I had fortunately repacked my own leather trunk and had put in my most valuable things, our real silver tea and coffee services, nearly all my jewellery, including my diamonds!! – bracelet, locket and brooch – sealskin cape and muff, and best white work. This was thrown out and remains with all its contents safe. The fur cloak you gave me, the clothes, houshold linen, children's things, books, pictures, toys, a most marvellous collection sufficient to fill a large linen chest and four large packing cases as full as they could hold were thrown out. We lost some things that were got out of the house, got burned because they could not be got out of the heat from the fire in time. A bookcase, 2 beds, 3 chairs, 2 tables was all the furniture saved besides all the bedclothes and 2 fur rugs. We had 3 clocks burnt, but my dear little carriage clock is safe in my good leather trunk. The two most valuable ones are saved. It was wonderful how much was saved considering the very few minutes it had to be done in. John lost at least 5 minutes in a very wise precaution when he saw the fire blowing towards the barn, he rushed to the stables and turned out the horses, and animals. You know horses will not move if a place gets on fire. We can get almost everything here. I have everything I want for the present, both for myself and for the children. I have only had to buy boots and shoes for us all, Sunday hats for the children and a waterproof for myself. John has also supplied his present needs. We have more than we want, and, as Mother used to say, 'A great deal more than we deserve.' Last Saturday week, very late in the afternoon Mr Ingalls drove over in his buggy – as the roads were almost impassible from the heavy rains on the previous days, both John and I were so apprehensive that he might be the bearer of bad news from home and had been deputed to break it to us. Instead of that he had met Mr. Crossley at Topeka and had brought such a beautiful letter from Mr. Crossley to John. I only regret that John has not kept the letter to send on to you. I cannot tell you how deeply touched both John and I were by its contents. I can give you no idea of the delicacy and beauty of the letter. I can only give you, as it were, the gist of it. He said he knew of our friends in England would make good our losses, but it took time for them to know, and he said he would place any amount at our disposal at his friend's, a banker in Eureka, so we might rebuild without delay. Then added regret we should have had trouble with our Insurance Policy, and asking as proof of friendship to accept the loan of the amount payable at sight in Heaven! or when we liked. John wrote saying friends had cabled placing money at our disposal, and our Insurance money, to our surprise, had suddenly without demand, been paid in full. I added a short note of thanks. I enclose his answer. I wish you could have seen his first letter, the way I have put it seems gauche and stupid. I fear they have had trouble as John surmised from previous rumours. Mr Kerr had eloped

Marian's sister-in-law Marianne Haworth, Jesse's wife

to Missouri, and Mrs Kerr has instituted divorce proceedings. You will, of course, not let this out of the family. I should be so very sorry to give information the Crossleys would rather not be known. Unfortunately such news cannot be kept back. The law here is that the wife can claim half of everything. I don't know how they have come out on money matters. When John was in England Mr Thompson sent for him to make enquiries, and said old Mrs Kerr was dreadfully anxious about her son, but John did not say anything as he was not sure of his authority. We shall only be too glad of any literature you can send us – books are a great treat. I try to read for an hour in the heat of the day. Flies make sleep an impossibility but with the aid of a fan I could have a very good read. Would you think it dreadfully commonplace if I asked you to send Chamber's Journal? There is no rubbish in it and a good deal of useful information for everyday life.

Give my dear love to Jesse and accept much from your ever loving sister,

Marian Whitworth

* Mr Armitage was Marianne Haworth's father.

Bowdon, Emporia, Kansas 21st August 1887
(Marian to her sister-in-law, Helena Whitworth)

My very dear Helena,

Many thanks for your kind letter, I was very pleased to hear about your Bowdon visit and especially about your new little godchild. I have no doubt the visit to Colwyn Bay will do Mother and Mary great good. Is Mrs. Cook stronger? Has Hannah* got married? I wonder how you and Miss Groom got on with your cooking experiences. I am chief cook and bread baker. Emma does not bake nor has any desire to learn. Our house is getting on very well. The masons left this week. The house looks good and substantial and quite imposing standing on the top of the hill, with other hills rising up behind it and the wood below. In comparison with the kind of wooden shanties called by the name of farmhouses we are very grand people round here. I have not been able to get John to make a sketch and plan of the house to send to you, but he promises to draw one for his mother. He is kept busy from 6 am until about 7 in the evening, then he seems too tired to settle to anything. He just loafs about like he used to do at Alderley looking at the poultry and animals, sometimes we go to bed a little after 9. 10 is our bedtime but they all seem tired and glad to get to rest. Nick is leaving us when the year he came for is expired, the beginning of October, he is a particularly nice lad, thoughtful, high principled and kind, but sometimes rather trying in his work. He is most anxious to do the right thing and in his nervousness and eagerness to do the best he generally does the wrong thing. I can well understand why his father should try Uncle Robert.** Mr Falconer has stayed with us all the time, there has been plenty of work for him. He has worked well and cheerfully, and has received no wage. At the fire Nick saved all his own things that were not at the back of the house where the fire first started, then saved what he could for us. Mr. Falconer tried to save all that he could for us and only at the very last did he rush to his room and threw some of his things out of the window and then had to jump out himself. We intend to make good his losses in clothes and, if he stays this winter which we hope he will, John will pay him wages. I wonder what arrangements your Father will make about Mr Walter Barrett*** coming to us. It is a very sad case and one longs to be of some use in trying to cure such a dreadful disease. If he should come, the difficulty about sending the winter socks you and Miss Groom have so kindly knitted for John will be solved. I should be glad if you could get me about 6 pr. of summer socks. What we buy here is such rubbish and do not wear at all. I should like about 2 doz. spoons, all our spoons were burnt, a box of knives and forks which Tom gave us for a wedding present was saved, so we are well off for forks, but all else went in the silver plate line. I bought 18 large spoons and 18 teaspoons but the silver is already wearing off and they look quite dark coloured. They make things for show, not for wear. They do not make any difference between table and dessert spoons: they split the difference and have about the size of soup spoons. Jack has a suit of clothes he will be able to wear next winter for Sundays, but I should like a strong suit of corduroy for him to wear about the farm. I bought both Jack and Walter corduroy suits to last for four winters but they got burnt. Walter has a suit that will fit him for next winter. These things depend on Mr. Barrett's coming. If any friend was coming to New York and would forward a parcel by Adam's Express that would be a good plan. Adam's corresponds with our Sutton; but being American of course is on a larger scale. If you can think of any way of sending them I will either ask them at home to send you the money, or I could send you Green Backs which you could get changed. The children all keep wonderfully well and are growing fast, but none as much as Walter, who is getting such a caution and a very mischief. I am always in fear he will be getting into some trouble, he knows no fear. I had another attack of that wretched Cholera Morbus, though not so severe it prostrated me dreadfully.

(The rest of this letter is missing)

* *Hannah was the daughter of Alfred Whitworth, John's uncle; she married a Mr Peak in Egypt.*

** *Robert Whitworth (1828–1901) was the younger brother of Benjamin Whitworth, John's father, who joined the firm Benjamin Whitworth and Brothers, cotton importers and manufacturers in Manchester. Like his brother he was an ardent teetotaller, a Liberal in politics and a well-known member of the Reform Club in Manchester. He was a tireless fundraiser for the Manchester branch of the RLNI and a lifeboat was named in his honour which was based at Whitby. He married Martha Walker, the younger sister of Benjamin's wife, Jane.*

*** *Walter Barrett was clearly an alcoholic whom Benjamin Whitworth was anxious to help. Kansas was a Prohibition State, and thus a very suitable place for such a person to go to break this addiction. It was also hoped that he could make himself useful on the farm.*

Emporia, Kansas 2nd September 1887
(Marian to her mother, Marianne Haworth)

My very dear Mother

I received Jesse's letter two days ago. When I opened it I saw the newspaper cutting and glanced at that first, knowing that you were staying at Miss Heyes'. I hardly knew what to read first, the letter or the account on the slip. The very name of fire seems to stop my heart beating. It seemed such a time before I could get to that part where Jesse spoke of your experience of the fire. I felt I could not be sufficiently thankful that all of you were safe, and that you, especially, were no worse for the shock. I am of course glad you saved your pocket and your belongings, but these seem paltry in comparison with what might have been lost. Sometimes I can hardly stifle regrets when I think of many treasures that went in our cruel fire, but I always come back to my anchor sheet – deep thankfulness that no life was lost or injured. Harriet's letter with a still fuller account of the fire came yesterday, please thank her for it. I am so sorry her pleasure trip to Ireland should have been so spoilt. I can quite sympathise with the painfulness and weakness of such an experience. Like me she will have to be very careful. I find any extra exertion such as walking or driving on these rough roads brings on an attack of diarrhoea. I had to pay for going to the service I told you about at Badger Creek. I have not been to town since my first attack, I hope to go next Sunday as John and I are to be received into the church at Emporia then. They do not receive members at the church meetings, but at the Communion Service. The church has been closed for the whole of the month of August. The children go to school on Monday. Daisy and Walter will go in the morning, the two elder ones for the whole day. We have not been able to make arrangements to send them into town; the Normal College and the High School have splendid buildings and teachers and each has a kindergarten attached. For the present we felt obliged to be content with the District School.* The School house is just across the road from our land, on the north. The teacher engaged has good certificates. Our man left us yesterday, I expect we shall miss him. John has not been very well these last two or three days – he has been able to do his work but it has felt an effort. I think it is his liver. He has been particularly well during the hot weather. I send you a small sketch of the house, John has drawn. I hope it may give you some idea of our new house. The work now seems to progress very slowly, the roof is not yet on, then the flooring, partitions have to be put up ready for the plasterers. We do hope the cold weather

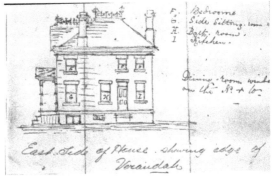

John Whitworth's pen sketches of the stone-built farmhouse, 1887, and photograph of the house in its setting, nearing completion.

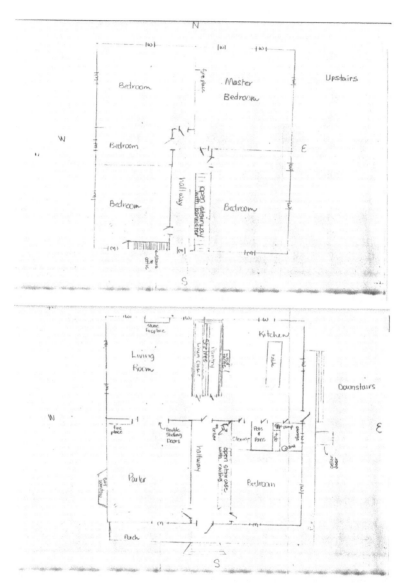

Plans of the layout of rooms as remembered by Mr Robert Korte

will not find us in this house. I see no chance of our getting into the other before the middle of October. We are imagining you all full of interest in the British Association meetings and the pleasure of seeing the many friends it will bring. We feel quite out of this Manchester red letter year,** still through you all we feel to have a share in it.

With much love to you each and all, believe me dear Mother, ever your loving -daughter, Marian.

The children attended the local common school of School District 71.

** *This was the year of the great Jubilee Exhibition and also saw the cutting of the first sod of the Manchester Ship Canal at Eastham by Lord Egerton. This was to link Manchester with Liverpool and the sea.*

No address, no date
(Mary Whitworth to her grandmother, Jane Whitworth)

My dear Grandmama,

I would also like to see you too. We are going to school now. The school house is only just across the field. We have three cats and we thought one of them was burnt in the fire because it went away for a long time and then it returned. We had a fire in the new house today to make ourselves warm. There is a little girl called Ellie Curtis who comes and plays with me and Daisy, who lives where Charlie used to live. They have gasoline stoves here. We are going to have open fireplaces in our new house. I feed the ducks and geese and chickens. Father made a man for Walter with a turnip. Father brought us a little wagon. I can milk one of the cows. It was very cold this morning. This cottage has only got three rooms in it. Our house is on a hill. The chickens with black and white feathers are called Plymouth Rocks. I have got two little white chickens which I set. Tell Uncle Ben that I send my love.

Your loving friend, Mary Whitworth.

Emporia, Sept 18th 1887
(John to his mother, Jane Whitworth)

My dear Mother,

I am glad to say now the weather has got cooler all the family are looking well, Marian especially seems quite herself again. Our new house is nearly ready for us, the plasterers are now at work and as soon as it is

61

*The newly finished farmhouse with Marian and
Gladys Whitworth standing outside*

dry enough we will get into it. It will be a nice comfortable roomy house.
We have large open fireplaces in two rooms for good sized logs so will
look quite cheerful. The children, except baby are all going to school and
seem to be getting on nicely. They are all growing like willows and seem
as happy as happy can be. Baby, Walter and May are especially fond of
animals; they fetch the cows up at milking time, have a pet lamb who
follows them about everywhere, in fact they are on the best of terms with
all the livestock. Baby has a pet colt, I often see her petting and kissing it.
We have had splendid rains lately and the grass looks as green and fresh as
it did in May. Nicholai is leaving us soon, his father thought he could not
make much out of farming as he could find him no capital to start with. He
is a nice lad but thoroughly Irish and not much account for hard work. He
is going to try for a place in Kansas City or Chicago but he has no business
ability at all – never saw a lad with less. I suppose father will have told
you about Mr. Barrett who is likely to come out to us, we like him very
much. We have no hired help now. The house keeps us very busy indeed;
we have to get a load from town almost daily. I do wish some of you could
come over when we get settled and see all our surroundings. I cannot hear

The storm shelter under construction

of any great improvement in business on your side, as for farming it never was so bad. I sold 4 fat cows this week for 1d lb live weight.

Your affec. Son,
John.

The new farmhouse and its surroundings

The view from the house over the farmyard and barn

THE LETTERS
PART III

1887–1888

Ecclesfield Sept 18th. 1887
(Walter Haworth to his sister Marian Whitworth)

My dear Polly,

I have received your welcome letter on September 5th., the day after my birthday, and I had previously posted a line to you on the morning of the same day on my way to the office. It is very pleasant to find you have not forgotten your youngest brother's birthday, and for all your good wishes I am very grateful. You were never 46 I believe, were you? The feeling is a bit queer.

And now my dear girl I have in a sense painful news to tell you, for yesterday at 12 o'clock noon, Saturday September 17th, our darling Mother quietly and very peacefully passed into the 'Better Land' – sister Harriet, Ellen, Alice Dyson and Marian were all at her side at the last moment, and so calm was the departure that they were hardly conscious it had taken place. Literally 'her end was peace'. We propose laying her at Father's side at Harpurhey on Wednesday Sept. 21st. Mr Mackennal will, we expect, conduct a little service here, and our old friend and pastor Mr. Bedell at the cemetery. We are inviting Hilston House, Woodside, Urmston people; Ada and her husband, Tom Falkner and Minnie, Uncle and Aunt Blakemore, Tom Haworth and wife, Alice Dyson, Robert and Mary Deacon. It is intended that the six grandsons – three Varley and three Haworths – shall carry their Grandmother to her last resting place – and what more can I say? You know what is in my heart, but I cannot speak it, much less write it. I am trying to think 'All's well' and I want you, dear Polly, to do the same, for after all as far as she's concerned, it is well. I cannot write more tonight. Some of the others will probably be saying something more fully about our Mother's last hours to you but I felt it fitting you should know of our Mother's departure from me first. Remember me to John, and kiss the children in my name.

Believe me, dear Polly, your affectionate brother, Walter.

Notice of Marianne Haworth's death:

In loving memory of
Marianne
widow of the late
Smallshaw Lomax Haworth
who entered into her rest on
Saturday September 17th 1887
aged 77 years.
'With Christ which is far better'.

Ecclesfield, Bowdon.

Bowdon, P.O.Box 1144, Emporia 9th October 1887
(Marian to her sister-in-law, Marianne Haworth)

My very dear Marianne,
We have not been to church today. It rained heavily yesterday. The roads here are hardened mud and in wet weather become extremely muddy and slushy. The soil, I suppose partly from its richness, is peculiarly sticky. You would hardly credit it without seeing it, how it sticks to everything when you walk through it. It seems as if it would drag the boots off your feet. Great clods of dirt stick to the shoes and though we had longed and prayed for rain last summer, it makes everything very dirty and disagreeable. I shall never forget the dreariness of the week before last – the proverb 'troubles never seem to come alone' was verified. The day I received Harriet's letter telling me Dr Cox seemed to consider dear Mother's case was hopeless, the rain came down in torrents. Our shanty which has stood us good service, and considering everything (is) very comfortable, was not proof against such rain. The walls became reeking with wet, and we had to keep moving our beds about to avoid rain which came dripping in through the shingles. The children were unable to go to school, or outside, and seemed very much in the way. Perhaps I felt it so much the more from being in such a state of terrible suspense about my darling. I have been spending today reading and re-reading all the letters relating to the last two weeks of her life and thinking about her, and though there are many things in your letters that bring a kind of balm and I try to think of her as safe, and I shall have no further cause for anxiety and suspense on her account, it is still a bitter and hard blow for me. For two or three days after receiving Walter's letter I felt as if I should almost go out of my mind to think her body had been lying in its last resting place 2 days before I received your first letter, which was the first intimation of any danger, and until I received your second letter and also Abms. and Harriet's I was almost rebellious. I kept asking myself why I should have been allowed to come, and she should be taken six months and a day afterwards, but since receiving all the details, I have felt the same as I did when I decided it was the right thing to do to come to America. Mother had such loving care around her. I was not necessary to her, like I was to John – and now when I know how she glided away in spite of all the loving care, I know I couldn't have done any more than was done, still the thought of not being any use does not always bring comfort with it. I so long to be with Walter. I gave Mother into your charge and now I must give Walter. I can do nothing but pray for him. The children seem happy at school. Daisy especially is very fond of it. She is a little go-ahead – first

up in the morning, first to go to school, first home, first in everything. Little Walter does not take at all kindly to school. He is taken with very violent and sudden pains at schooltime, and is so ill that tears will come in his eyes! He gets home from school at dinner time when the others are starting back, always having come to grief in some way accidentally on purpose! I have to be my firmest and sternest. He tries all sorts of arts and ruses to evade going. Thank you so much for the wreaths, it is quite a comfort to feel that my loss and the children's had an outward expression; and also for the sympathy, which was very precious to me.

With fondest love to you and Jesse, I am always, dear Marianne, your loving sister, Marian.

Please give Harriet my love and tell her I hope to write in a few days.

Marianne Haworth, Marian's mother, died intestate on 17 Sept. 1887; her personal estate amounted to £760. 16s. 2d.

Bowdon, Emporia, Kansas 19th October 1887
(Marian to her mother-in-law, Jane Whitworth)

My dear Mother,

Very many thanks for your kind letter of sympathy. The death of my darling Mother has been a sad blow to me. I know what is my loss is her gain, but oh it is so hard to be unselfish and look on the immortal side. I feel I could have borne it so much better if I could have been with her to the very end: perhaps not. I must be very thankful for her life and try to make my own what she would have wished. Having lost her makes me long more for what is left. I long to be near you, to heap some of the loving care I would so gladly have given to make your life brighter and surround you with loving attentions. I do trust you will be spared us for a very long time, that we may see you often. It makes the world so desolate when those who have made home for us are taken. There are many things in connexion with the end of my mother's earthly life which will be an increasing comfort for me to think about. She was out for a drive on the Saturday before she died, was downstairs on the Sunday, and sat up in her bedroom on Thursday and wanted to get up on Friday. She attempted to get up several times, but found herself too weak. She was very restless all Friday night, on Saturday morning my niece went into her room and said 'Good morning, Grandma,' and she replied 'Good morning love, good morning, give me a little cold water.' My niece gave her a teaspoonful and she fell into a sweet sleep. My brother, Walter, went in to see her before starting for town, and thought he would see her refreshed and better when he returned at noon, she seemed to be resting so beautifully she slept on. My sister, niece, Mrs Jesse and our cousin Mrs Dyson were all round her bed about a quarter to twelve they noticed a change in her breathing, and waited for the next sigh which never came, so calmly did she pass the borderland. They could not believe, but she would not open her eyes and smile on them. The servants asked if they might not do what was necessary, and assisted by Mrs Dyson they did, and she lay in quiet state in a very bower of flowers. She was carried to her last resting place by six grandsons: 3 of Abm's* and 3 of Harriet's* boys, no hirelings hand ever touched her. That comforts me so much. My niece, Lily, made a lovely cross, and put on it 'For the dear grandchildren across the seas - Mary, John, Daisy, Walter and baby Gladys Whitworth.' Mrs Jesse* made a wreath for me 'For the absent one,' and also another for the children. I do feel so grateful that our loss and grief should have been represented. They tried to bring us into everything. There was a service in the drawing room in which Mr Mackennal seemed to have us in mind all the time. Mr. Bedell, an old friend and my Mother's minister nearly 30 years ago took the service at the cemetery, Harpurhey, where she was laid to rest beside her husband, who went before her 29 years ago. My niece, Harriet,* said it was such a comfort to see the grave. There was a door at the foot which seemed to lead into a kind of little room, neither the stone nor the flowers on top were the least bit disturbed as my nephews lowered the coffin. Men inside just took it and tenderly placed it in. Nellie** was at Ecclesfield. A few pieces of fern and flowers fell from the coffin as my nephews brought it downstairs. Nellie pressed them and sent them on to me.

Thank you so much for sending those things with Mr. Barrett. I do hope all that his friends hoped for will be attained by his coming here - if so we shall be thankful our coming here was not in vain. I do wish you could see our new house...

(The rest of this letter is missing)

* See the Haworth family tree. Abraham Haworth (1830–1902) and Harriet Varley née Haworth (1840–1915) were Marian Whitworth's eldest brother and sister. Mrs Jesse was Marianne Haworth (1841–1936), the youngest daughter of Mr William Armitage; she was married to their brother, Jesse (1835–1920). Marian's niece, Harriet Varley, daughter of her elder sister Harriet, went out to visit the family in Kansas before she married Mr Ford.

*** Nellie Kirkpatrick, née Clarke, was Marian Whitworth's nursemaid at*
Glebelands, Bowdon, before the family emigrated to America.

Emporia Oct. 25th 1887
(John to his mother, Jane Whitworth)

My dear Mother,
  I am writing this in the Dining Room of our new house and exceedingly comfortable it promises to be. Mr. Schofield and Mr. Barrett arrived here on Sunday, the former left us on Monday as he had engagements to fulfill. We like him very much indeed and would have liked him to stay longer. He promised to call on you on his return and tell you about our surroundings and how he found us all. Mr. Barrett brought us a present of some delicious tea, a real treat I can assure you. We get splendid coffee here but could not get decent tea at any price. We are much obliged for things sent, we have not yet seen them as Mr. B's case, in which they are, has not yet arrived. weather has become quite cool, it seems to suit Marian better than the hot weather. The children are all first rate. Little Walter especially bids fair to be the strongest of the family. They are getting on nicely at school. Daisy is making good progress and seems to like school very much. Walter is a dunce at school but sharp enough for two outside. He only goes in the morning. He has been one month learning how to spell cat.

Dear Mother, John is such a dreadful letter writer, when I said I should like to add a word or two to his letter, he came to an abrupt termination. Thank you so much for your kindness in sending the things with Mr. Barrett, so far we only got the pinafores and some delicious tea Mr. Barrett bought...

(The rest of this letter is missing)

Bowdon, Emporia, Kansas 10th December 1887
(Marian to her mother-in-law, Jane Whitworth)

My dear Mother,
  Christmas is not thought much of in these parts, it is not even a holiday. The only recognized holidays are Independence Day, 4th July, and Thanksgiving Day (the last Thursday in November). Though in America we are still English and shall be very near you all in heart and

spirit on Christmas Day, and will send you greetings as truly as if they were cards or any other orthodox way. I shall be glad if you will send on this letter to Aunt Jane,* I had a most kind letter from her two or three days ago and which I should like to answer in full, had I the time and I know in her unselfishness she would rather I did not make any special effort to get in a separate letter to her. She says she would like to know details of our life, so that she can imagine our surroundings. I will try to give you an idea of the ordinary routine of my week's work. We do not get up very early this weather. We try to have breakfast as near 7 as possible. I first sweep and dust the dining room after breakfast. (I don't do anything before except to help Emma with the breakfast if she is late). Then I get the children ready for school, after skim the milk and put the morning's milk away. On Monday Emma washes, I do all the housework, cooking, and folding the clothes in the afternoon. I never take her off the washing for a single thing. She does not begin to wash till after breakfast and finishes from 5 to 6. I get tea and put the children to bed. She washes up the tea things and goes to bed _before_ 8. She has to carry all the water in buckets from outside: as yet we have no taps in the house. On Tuesday I bake, make pastry and get the dinner under way, Emma always prepares the vegetables except on Mondays. I am busy until dinner time, which is 12 prompt, that is the universal dinner hour. Aunt Jane* wonders if we can buy bread – not nearer than the town. When I was ill in the summer and they were hauling things every day for the house we bought bread, a 10 cent loaf weighs 1 1/4 lbs, sometimes only 1 lb. It used to cost about $4 a week for bread, a sack of flour weighing 98lbs. lasts us for pastry, bread and everything for a fortnight and costs $2.40 rather a difference. The yeast is in very convenient form, in hard cakes, and will keep quite well for a year. It takes longer to rise both in the sponge and afterwards. I always put it to sponge overnight, and bake two or three times a week, and always make a little brown bread as well. Brown flour is called Graham Flour. I have been very successful with bread. We have a splendid cooking stove which we bought when we came into this house. It is both handsome in its looks and ways, so easy to clean and to manipulate; better than any kitchen range I had to do with in England. It has 6 holes for pans, a boiler and a warming cupboard, the oven works splendidly. We have only open fireplaces in the two sitting rooms and even in these we have a separate flue for stoves should the weather be too cold for anything but stoves. John does enjoy the log fires, they are very cheerful, but take an amount of wood to keep going. We have stone mantelpieces made by an English marble-mason in town, with stone hearth and a kind of stone fender. Had we not been so afraid of fire we should have had pretty carved wood ones, but these are much safer and look well. To return to household work

– Wednesday, I churn and finish the ironing Emma left undone on Tuesday, she always irons the collars and John's white shirt which is only worn on Sundays, and does not come into the wash oftener than every two or three weeks. I do the other ironing. Thursday I generally have to bake, and Saturday is a very busy day getting ready the Sunday's cooking, as well as the Saturday's. We take it in turn to watch the dinner cooking whilst the others go to church. John takes his turn, and Nick and Mr Falconer together. Nick is very like a girl and can manage very well in the house. Mr. Falconer cannot, and would not be left in charge on any consideration. I find something to do after dinner, either in getting ready for tea, or supper as it is called here, which is at 6. We always have some hot meat of some kind, except on Sunday, but we do not always have vegetables. Men working outside, especially in this exhilarating air want substantial food. We live very much like we did in England. We always begin breakfast with porridge, or ceraline boiled in milk, but once a week we copy the Americans and have pancakes. Americans have them every morning, besides other hot bread, then we have bacon, or sausage, or mutton chops. Dinner we have meat, potatoes and some other vegetable either carrot, turnip, squash, pumpkin or cabbage or beetroot. Then we have some sort of milk pudding, and a boiled pudding, or a pie, we try to give as much variety as we can in them. John usually comes in about 4 o'clock in the afternoon and I make him a cup of tea. We both greatly enjoy this especially since we got the English tea. Mr. Barrett has ordered a chest for us and is certain it will not cost more than we pay here. The children come home from school at 4.30. I get their tea ready and then it is almost time for the other tea to be got ready. After supper is over and the children are in bed. The two elder children put themselves to bed and bath themselves all over twice a week. The little ones are bathed every night. Daisy can almost manage herself. I find the mending for 10 people takes me always until prayer time which is 9.30, after that we have a glass of hot milk and go to bed at 10 o'clock. On Sunday afternoon I usually get an hour or two for quiet reading. I daresay you will think this is a busy life. I think so but then I think that life here would simply be unbearable were it not for its business. Since we came to this house I have been very well and quite enjoy the work. Emma, the girl, is clean and a capable servant, but rather uncertain in temper, on the whole we get along very well by my letting her have very much her own way. The menkind are very busy with the outside work, the heaviest falls on John. We have no hired man this winter, John ploughs etc. but he is just as happy as happy can be, is in splendid health and enjoys life to the fullest extent. The children are in capital health. May and Jack can ride bare-back. Walter wants to but is not allowed. The other week I took him out to watch his father breaking a colt,

John Whitworth and his sons; Marian Whitworth and her daughters

he looked very much disappointed as he watched, at length he said 'I did not think Father breaked them that way, I thought he broke them in pieces.'

The other morning I had a cup of coffee before getting up. Baby and Walter came to watch. Baby said 'Walter is tasting'; I said 'I'll taste him'. 'No', he said, 'you cannot I'se too sweet, I'd make you sick. I'se sweeter than sugar!' John says this house is incomparably warmer than the one that was burnt down. It is very convenient and comfortable. The weather, with the exception of two days, has been warm. One of the cold days it was 2 degrees below zero, but was not so cold as the day before when we had a blizzard and only 14 degrees of frost.

With every good wish of the season to all and each,
I am always dear Mother, your loving daughter,
M.Whitworth, The children send their kisses.

Aunt Jane was Benjamin Whitworth's unmarried sister.

Emporia December 29th 1887 (John to his Mother, Jane Whitworth)

My dear Mother,

This will be rather late to wish you either a Happy Christmas or New Year, but if it gets posted pretty promptly it may be in time for your Birthday and to wish you many happy returns. Winter is now fairly on us, last night it was 4 below zero. The children were rather out of sorts last week, I think they had been playing in the snow and caught cold but they are now all right again. Daisy is very fond of school and can read a little. Jack took one out of two prizes given at the school. Walter so far is a little dunce, he likes to play too much but he is as bright and happy as possible and a general favourite. I can tell you he grows faster than any of them and is getting quite stout. Baby lost flesh in the hot weather, but is now as fat as ever. Marian has had a sore throat for a day or two but is decidedly better today. Weather being so cold we don't see much company just now but with Mr. Falconer, Nick, Mr. Barrett and myself we never feel lonely. Sometimes we have a game of whist and we all read a good deal. Mr. Barrett looks quite a different person, looks wonderfully healthy, has a splendid appetite and is gradually dropping into our ways. He cannot be called fond of work by any means, in fact as a farm hand he is not worth his board. At first he rather seemed to look on this place as a kind of hotel where he could do and order as he liked, but he has found out his mistake. He has never spoken about his old failing indeed we hardly think he knows that we know all about it. I am quite sure that since he came here he has been a total abstainer, but should not like to trust him where it could be obtained.* Nick may leave us any day as his Father thinks of having him back again in Drogheda. We were going to a very nice neighbours; Marian for the day with the wife, me for a day's shooting with the husband, but the weather being so cold we have had to postpone it. They are well educated eastern people and about our own age. How we would like to drop in and see you all. Let us hear from you often by letter please. Our Minister, Mr Ingalls, my best friend in Emporia, is leaving here to become president of a college in Missouri. We shall feel quite lost without him.**

With best love to all, Your affec. son, John

Marian sends her love and birthday greetings, will write again soon.

* *William Mackennal remarks in his biography of John H. Whitworth that 'Many inebriates were sent to Kansas to be cured, and their intense demand for alcohol sometimes succeeded in attracting an illicit supply'. He may have been referring to Mr. Barrett.*

**Dr Frank J. Ingalls became President of Drury College, Missouri.*

Emporia, Kansas, 15 Jany 1888
(Marian to her sister-in-law, Marianne Haworth)

My very dear Marianne,

Thank you very much for your last two letters. The last I received on the 10th. I was so anxious to know how you spent Christmas Day. I tried to picture you all, for one thing I could not be certain if you would keep it on Saturday or Monday though I imagined the latter. I rejoice you all had such a happy time, I am also certain our dear one would. Had I been able to express what I should wish – it would be those beautiful lines you quoted of Whittier. I did my best to make the day bright and cheery both for John's sake and the children, but I could not help feeling heart-loneliness, and an intense craving for the sight of home faces.

Your letter and Harriet's telling me of what had been done with Mother's things seemed like the opening of unclosed wounds. I could not bear it. Every single article had a separate memory. Since I have been married Mother did not buy anything for herself. Before I was more like her sister and friend, we only had each other. I could tell you where each thing was bought, when and the price. The sable muff that is being saved for me she bought the winter before I went to Culchett (?), I was just a little over Mary's age. She bought it at a furrier called Hanck at the end of

King St.(*Manchester*) next to where the Swiss shop is. I was with her, she gave £6.6s.8d. for it, she thought it was very extravagant. I remember her saying it would last her life. The tippet she bought the next winter at Kendal Milnes but she was not very satisfied with it as the quality was not so good. In the same way I could go over all the different things. Her dear wedding ring she two or three times said to me she would like to be buried with her – it must now be buried with me instead. The silk jacket you have given me I think I would like Aunt Dolly to have. She was so proud of Mother and so devoted to her – if she does not wear it out I would like her daughter, Jane, to have it. If Harriet Ellen has been led to think she is to have Mother's brooch, she had better have it. I should not like her to be disappointed – if not I should like it. You said in one of your letters now we have got a good house I should miss all the pretty things we bought out with us, and had been lost in the fire. I do not allow myself to talk about what we lost, I try not even to think about it, and be so thankful for the great mercies we had through all. I did not quite know how great our losses were until I could really unpack everything. It was impossible when the salvage was put in the barn to sort out and make a complete list of everything amidst the litter and the upset of the barn. The only thing was to try to get everything for our immediate wants and find places for them in the shanty, and get the remainder nailed up in boxes as quickly as possible, lest they should be completely spoiled. In spite of all precaution the mice made sad havoc with the books. Two or three pieces of jewellery I imagined were in a box in my leather trunk that was saved, I found had been packed in the silver chest that was burnt. We had a kind of silver box with shelves for plated silver, of which we had quite a store. Now we use German silver. My whole stock of jewels consists of my diamond ring, a small ring Mother gave me, also a gold brooch given by her, a gold locket she gave me, with a chain Bessie gave me when I was married, a gold bracelet of (?) work. This is my entire stock – far more than my present requirements, still our three girls might prize indeed a piece of jewellery that belonged to their Grandmother. Everyone was congratulating themselves we had got through the winter very well. It has been unusually warm. We have had cold snatches once 4 degrees, another 7 degrees below zero, but the cold soon passed and kept changing from about 20 degrees of frost to 40 or 50 above (*freezing*). But on Thursday a terrible blizzard came on. You cannot imagine the terribleness of these violent piercing N.W. winds called blizzards. While the wind was raging from Thursday until Saturday it was 10 degrees below zero, it was impossible to keep warm besides the inconvenience of every single thing being frozen – even when the stove was lighted – milk solid, bread having almost to be chopped, your breath freezing on the sheets and pillowslips, everything you touched being like ice itself. Yesterday the wind disappeared and though it was 20 degrees below zero because the air was still the cold was much more bearable. Today we have ceased to shiver and shake, and feel that life may be endured. This morning it was only 2 degrees below zero, and tonight it is 12 above. I do trust we have seen the worst. Friday and Saturday were the climax - the end of January is supposed to see the end of the severe weather. John has not borne the cold weather at all well. I was rather uneasy about him last week. His liver I think was out of order and he looked very ill and complained of faintness and weakness. A red lump came up on his leg – it looked like the beginning of a boil – but it is passing away very nicely and he seems to be regaining his strength. Baby has had both her heels bad with broken chillblains. I think the frost must have got in them, they have gathered and been very painful. She stayed in bed for a week, I daresay it was the best thing for her but it seemed unnatural. I think her feet will soon be alright – they are healing nicely. I have not liked the cold still I have kept well, this has been a mercy especially as the girl, Emma, has been a coward with the cold and has gone about wringing her hands and saying 'Oh dear, oh dear, if ever I get back to England I will never complain or say it is cold!!!' I certainly should not have liked to come downstairs and found everything frozen, even the water left in the kettle on the stove, frozen solid, and had to light the fires. I hope Jesse is stronger and better. I can quite understand how Lily would enjoy being with you in Southport. Having experienced your good nursing and coddling, I know what it is. I had a most delightful long letter from her, tell her with my love I will answer as soon as I have time.

Give my love also to each member of the home circle, you and Jesse accepting a full share, and love, dear Marianne, believe me your loving sister, Marian Whitworth.

Emporia P.O.Box 1144 17th January 1888
(Marian Whitworth to her Mother-in-law, Jane Whitworth)

My dear Mother,
Mr Barrett's boxes have at length arrived. I have personal satisfaction in their safe arrival, as I am much richer by it. Will you all please accept my best thanks, Helena, Bessie and Mary. The only thing I have to say is they are all too good. I have already used the teaspoons – a Col. and Mrs Steele* from Emporia came out to call upon us. I made them afternoon tea and used the teaspoons and the pretty china Janie gave us for our wedding, it is the only china saved from the fire, of all that we bought out with us.

Tell Bessie Jack looks such a swell in his corduroys, they fit him like a skin, and are only just large enough, they will not fit him next winter, but will be a capital suit for Walter when he is old enough. The pillow slips are very swell, you must have been very busy. Helena's merino socks that were sent for John will have to be kept for Sundays and holidays. Fancy him doing farm work in such beauties. He does not wear socks very lightly, they could not have a very long life. I cannot imagine how it is that you have not received more letters from us. I know John has written 3 times to you since Mr. Barrett came, if not more. I also wrote 3 times before the letter which was partly in answer to Aunt Jane's and which Mary tells me, in a letter received about a week ago, you have received. I will again please thank Mary for the nightdresses, they are very pretty and warm. The (*sewing things*) are also very useful, that sort of thing is very dear here, needles especially. I paid 10 cents for a thimble, you could buy 4 for a penny in England. I should think I had more than 20 thimbles, they all went in the fire. I am glad Mary had Miss Groome with her, some people always seem to have people with them to help them out of their troubles, and other people always seem to act the friend in need. We have had terrible cold spells, though I suppose on the whole the winter has not been a severe one. John has not seemed to stand the cold weather very well. At one time it seemed as if we were going to have a very sick house. Walter had a bright red rash which seemed as if it must be scarlet fever - but he had no sore throat or other ailment or symptom. Baby was poorly with nothing specially the matter as far as we could see, but did not want to get out of bed, and ate hardly anything – she has two broken chillblains, one on each heel, they have been very bad but are getting better slowly. John had one of his liver attacks but what alarmed me the most was the large red hard lump come on his leg, it seemed far too bad to be a boil. I felt certain it must be a carbuncle. The weather was at its worst, neither John nor any of our clan could go to town to see a doctor, but in two or three days it went away just as it came. You can't tell what a relief it was. Mr. Barrett, who has dipped into medicine, like he has into almost every subject, pronounced it a sort of skin disease with a very long name. You ask me how I like Mr. Barrett, if I am perfectly frank I should say I don't think I ever had such contempt for anyone. He is lazy and self-indulgent to a degree, and is the greediest man I ever saw. If we have any specially nice dish for pudding he hardly allows himself time to eat it, so that he may have a second helping. I do not exaggerate when I say he takes quite 1/4lb of butter to his <u>breakfast,</u> he eats more butter than bread, and that with bacon and sausage. He is a most intelligent and well-read man, and quite a philosopher, but I have not much hope for his ultimate recovery from his weakness, because I think self-denial is an unknown quality in his composition. I would far rather have all your troubles than a son like him, from what he says, only one of his six brothers is doing any good: you see other people have troubles.

January 25th. I was not able to finish this letter. I am very glad to be able to give a better account of everyone. John seems himself again. The children are alright, excepting Daisy who has a little cold but hardly worth mentioning, and we all feel glad we are getting to the end of January, because that sees the end of the intense cold. We have had it as low as 18 degrees below zero, but that was nothing compared to 10 degrees below zero with a blizzard. Anything more terrible than a blizzard cannot be imagined, it is a N.W. wind said to blow from the Rockies, piercing is not the word for it, it penetrates to your very marrow even in the house. I can't say I enjoy the great cold though I have enjoyed being out at zero with no wind and bright sunshine. Your breath forms icicles on the pillow slips and sheets, milk and everything frozen solid cannot be called pleasant, but I have been very well through it all, indeed better than I have been since my first attack of illness in June.

We had a very quiet Christmas, I was so glad it was Sunday, it was very hard for me to keep cheery and bright with so many memories crowding upon me. But I know she would wish us all to be happy....... I think I have told you what a sad loss we had in our minister, Mr.Ingalls, leaving us. Since he left we see from the papers his brother, the senator, has had his house totally destroyed by fire. We have not been to church since he left owing to the state of the weather. I do trust we may be fortunate in his successor. There is so little outwardly to promote religious life and growth here.

With fond love to each and all, I am always, dear Mother, your loving daughter,

Marian Whitworth.

Col. and Mrs Jas. Steele from South Carolina are mentioned in the 1886 Directory of Emporia as living at 35 Congress St., and he is described as a labourer.

Emporia March 6th 1888
(John and Marian to John's mother, Jane Whitworth)

My dear Mother,
This is Nick's last night with us; he leaves us tomorrow to try his luck in the world. We are very sorry to part with him, indeed it feels very like sending one of our children away. He will try and find some employment

in Topeka, only a short distance away, if so, we will see him from time to time. Cold weather has returned again after quite a warm spell, but not at all severe this time. School has already closed for the children, it only lasted 6 months this time, but we hope to have more next year. We are letting them have a fortnight's holiday, then a neighbour's daughter, who is going to be a teacher, will come for 3 months so they will get along pretty well. Daisy has made good progress and will be able to write you a letter before very long. She has such quaint sayings. She was looking at a book of animals the other night, she found some very curious ones she had never seen before and remarked that God did not know how to make them properly that time. Walter is an awful coon and

Nicholai Whitworth, Buenos Aires 'with kindest rememberances and love to Mrs John and all'

gets over his mother finely. He was the prime favourite at school when his teacher called him up, she told us all the children stopped their lessons till he had finished. They all look in splendid health just now and Marian is getting quite stout. We hope Walter and Henry Thomson may pay us a visit next summer, at any rate the latter writes me he will come if he can persuade Walter. We have had more rain than usual and feel hopeful of good crops this year. Last year the drought did a great deal of harm. We are gradually getting the House into decent shape, the masons left it in an awful mess, hardly expect to get it right this summer. I am planting creepers but it will take some time before the newness to wears off.

Dear Mother,

John says he knows I want to write to you and has left me to finish his letter. I am sure you cannot possibly have got all the letters we have written to you. We have rarely missed two weeks without writing to you. John and the children are well, I am better than I have been since I came, I have stood the cold very well. John is very busy and I don't think there is a happier man in Kansas than he is, happy in his work, and happy having his children around him. He is full of hope and full of plans for improving the place. I do wish you could see it, you would be so pleased with it. We are feeling quite low spirited about parting with Nick, he is a very nice, kind-hearted boy, will do anything for anyone if they are kind to him, but very obstinate if crossed. He has not the qualities to ensure business success, but he is a high principled boy. I hope you received the letter telling about the safe arrival of the things you so kindly sent by Mr. Barrett. On Friday we received the chest of tea which Mr. Barrett had ordered for us. It is 40lbs and cost us 3/3d per pound. There is no duty on tea. I cannot say that Mr. Barrett 'grows' on me; no doubt he is intelligent and clever but so utterly selfish and indolent you cannot have one iota of respect for him. Today we had a specially rich cake. He spread it an inch thick with butter. I hope our scheme of teaching the children will work out well. Miss Eldridge will come on Monday and stay in the house until Friday afternoon. The children are great fun – baby and Walter were quarrelling about a pencil. Baby said 'I shall tell God not to love you if you don't give me that pencil.' I like John saying Walter gets over me, not half as much as he gets over his father, sometimes I almost feel afraid John dotes on him so. John says look at the time, we have to get up early tomorrow, so with very much love I am, dear Mother, your loving daughter, Marian.

Please thank Helena for her letter, I hope to answer it soon. I am glad your domestic arrangements work smoothly; Jane has not parted with Alice has she?

Emporia April 18th 1888
(John Whitworth to his mother, Jane Whitworth)

My dear Mother,

I have not heard from any of you for a considerable time. We are all quite well, the children look as bright and jolly as we could possibly wish; and are growing very fast. Our country school has only 6 months school this year so Marian and I thought it best to get someone to teach them at home for three months longer. We found a very nice girl, a neighbour's daughter who was qualifying for a teacher, who was glad to come for 10$ a month. The children seem to be getting on nicely. When Jack and May can safely be trusted to drive, we intend sending them to the Normal College in Emporia where they can get a splendid education. They have about 800 students now. I suppose you have heard of Walter's journey round the world, he intends paying us a visit in June on his way home across America. Marian is quite excited at the prospect of seeing him. The country looks beautiful just now, the apples and cherries are in full bloom. We have had a splendid spring so far, plenty of nice showers and everything looks fresh and green. We have got some corn planted and are exceedingly busy. I wish you could see us in our new home. Walter will tell you what it is like if you see him. The girl we brought out with us left us without a moments notice; luckily we have found a nice amiable girl, rather slow, but we must consider ourselves lucky to get her as help is very scarce out here.

With best love to all at home, in which Marian joins me.

Your loving son, John.

Emporia 18th April 1888
(Marian Whitworth to her mother-in-law, Jane Whitworth)

My dear Mother,

I don't like John sending a letter without adding a few words. I am more busy than ever. Emma, the girl who came out with me, left us three weeks tomorrow. She had her mind very much poisoned by people telling her what a slave she was, and no American girl would do what she did, and she could easily get 5$ a week for the same work etc. etc. She certainly was the quickest and most capable servant I ever had, and in many ways a very valuable help – bright, good with the children and thoroughly respectable and trustworthy, but she had at times the most ungovernable and unreasonable temper. Once she got into a great rage with me because I washed out a churn I had asked her to wash and which she had left undone. She said she would leave then and went into town and half engaged a situation, but she thought better of it. Since then I have taken great care not to cross her, and let her have her own way. When Nick was here he and she used to quarrel most dreadfully. She used to get almost mad with rage: then she would have a cry and then would be as bright and right as possible. After he went she had no one to quarrel with and act as a safety valve. For a week or two she had been in a state of suppressed rage before she went, I pretended to be in utter ignorance of it, she could find no outlet for her temper. On Daisy's birthday, 29th. March, I had promised to take May and Daisy into town for a birthday treat. When I was getting ready Emma asked me to get her a Kansas City paper as she wished to look for advertisements: she thought it would be better for us both to have a change. I tried to reason with her, she said a friend has been told by one of Mrs. Jesse's servants that she set the house on fire. I told her that no-one could think that she had any intention of setting the house on fire, but she must admit she had been very careless. I got May and Daisy ready and was just ready to start myself when she came to me white with rage, and said she was not going to have the burning of the house reaped up against her and that she was going that very minute, and before I could recover my breath, I was so dumbfounded, she was out of the house and on her way through the cornfields to town. I had to take off my things, wash the breakfast things and get a very scratch kind of dinner. Miss (Myrtle) Eldridge, who teaches the children, drove me and the children for miles.

We scoured the countryside asking everybody and were returning very low-spirited at dusk having been more than 20 miles altogether when we met a farmer who lives about two miles from here. He told us that there were some people who had come to the next farm to his, and the sister of the lady had said she was willing to hire out for a month or two: we went there and engaged the girl to come the next day. Their home is in Ohio, she came out to Kansas to visit her sister, she is returning home in the autumn, and guesses she wont work in the hot weather! I do hope she will stay with me while Walter has been and gone, you have no idea the difficulty of getting a girl here. I have heard of several people who have driven for days all around the country, for a week at a time and not been able to hear of anyone, and one lady in town told me she had 6 in one month. It is rather easier to get help in the town, the girls do not like coming out. There is rather a dearth of the female sex: there are 3 men to one woman in Kansas. Emma came back for her things and her money. I think she was surprised I had got anyone. I think she expected me to go down on my knees and entreat her to stay at any price. The girl is very different from an English servant, of course, she has all her meals with us and is very much at home, she is very willing and amiable, but she is slow and not very reliable. I have a great deal more to do than with Emma. She does things which would jar with an English servant, for instance when we are making the beds she will go to the glass and consult me as to the style of her hair!! I cannot tell you how delighted I am at the thought of Walter coming, sometimes I feel quite sick with longing to have a sight of him. Next week we are having the painters to paint the outside of the house and do some inside work, I want to have things as nice as we can so that he will not think we are outside the limits of civilized life. Mr. Barrett's brother is thinking of coming out and trying life as a Kansas farmer. Mr. B. will go into partnership with him – anyone more unsuitable I don't know. He is rather improving though, but work is against his nature.

With much love to you all, dear Mother, your loving daughter, Marian Whitworth.

Emporia, Kansas, Box 1144,

2aq 17th May 1888
(May Whitworth to her Grandmother, Jane Whitworth)

My dear Grandmother,
I thank you very much for your last letter. I had a letter from Molly and Helen* about a fortnight ago and Jack had one from Helen. I suppose you are having nice weather now, it is so nice here now and there are so many

wild flowers here now, we have the wild Sweet William. We have a young lady who teaches us and her name is Myrtle Eldridge. We have another Nellie Clarke** now. I hope you are keeping well. Baby has such very curly hair and it curls lots better when it is not done than when it is done, but it is so knotty. We have had our house painted a week ago tomorrow and one of the painters went to town before he had done any work. We have some little turkeys, ducks and chickens. Some of our hens are dying of an illness and we are not getting many hens eggs because they are nearly all wanting to sit. One hen has got eleven chickens, but she had fourteen, but three got drowned. She had fifteen eggs. They are about six weeks old now. The people never say fortnight here but always say two weeks, if you say fortnight to them they ask how many weeks it is. Today is Sunday morning. Gladys Hope, the cow, has got a large calf, she is often named. I hope you are all well, and I send my love. Write soon.

Your loving granddaughter, May Whitworth.

Give my love to Grandfather.

(Added by Marian Whitworth)

Love to all, John intended to write to Mr. Whitworth for his birthday, but the man is going at once to town. Will write in a day or two. We are all well, hope you are the same, Ever your loving Marian.

* *Molly and Helen were the elder daughters of Mary (née Whitworth) and James Boyd, and were May and Jack Whitworth's cousins.*

** *Nellie Clarke (later Kirkpatrick) was the family's maid at Glebelands, Bowdon before they left for America.*

Walter Haworth clearly visited John and Marian and their family in June/ July 1888, although no letters survive describing the visit. It would have been particularly enjoyed by Marian who was very close to her brother.

Emporia, Kansas U.S. 16th August 1888
(Marian to Bessie Haworth, the wife of her brother Abraham)

My dear Bessie,

I thank you very much for writing to me about Marianne's illness. Though I was most anxious until I heard danger was past, it was a comfort to feel whatever was going wrong, I was to know about it, and not have it kept back. Though farther away, the home life seems more to me than ever. I had a letter from Marianne – she tells me of the sudden death of Miss Margaret, it would be a great shock to you. I am especially sorry for Miss Annie, she has devoted her life to her sister; it will be a great blank and a wrench.

I was wishing all July I could send you some of our heat and sunshine: if we could have equalled matters it would have been much pleasanter for both. The heat was intense, on the north wall of our house outside the thermometer stood one afternoon at 107 degrees: for about three weeks in the same place it hovered about 100 degrees in the middle of the day, sometimes a little under, but oftener over by one or two degrees. I found it most trying. I felt as if I was recovering from an illness, and could hardly drag about. The nights are generally cool here, but two or three nights we just lay outside the bed, and then it almost felt as if we were lying on top of a stove. The children have stood the heat wonderfully. Little Walter sometimes looked rather white and drooping: their energy is quite a wonder to me, always ready to run about and play when the perspiration is running down their faces. We had rain the beginning of this month, and since then it has been much cooler, indeed quite bearable. I have not been away from the house since Walter left, until last week when John took me to see a lady doctor in town. She has put me under treatment and I hope soon to feel the benefit from it.

Had we had the rain in July the corn crop would have been an unusually fine one, but taking everything together John says this is the best season he has had since he came to America. Mr. Barrett has left us. We feel quite a small quiet family, but he is no loss. The girl I have is Welsh, she has been in Iowa 7 years, she is only 18, good natured but rather a muddler and I have to pay her $3 a week – $4 is a very usual thing and in Kansas City and other large towns I hear that $5 is given and then I should not think the help taken was as good as one could get in England for £16 a year.

I hope Abm. is sleeping better, and keeping well. Lily will be very glad she was able to go to Scotland to see her Aunt. Tell her with my love I should be so glad if she would show her sympathy for the heat I have gone through and write me another letter!! If you don't think Alfie quite strong after his Swiss tour, you had better let Kansas finish the cure, we would take all the care we could of him.

With love to all, ever your affectionate sister, Marian Whitworth.

There follows a gap in the correspondence until 1890. In June 1889 John Whitworth added considerably to his property by purchasing the S.W.

Quarter of Section 4 Township 19 (some 159 acres) from Returah Kirkpatrick, a widow, for $2,385. The land lay behind the schoolhouse which the Whitworth children attended (S.D. 71), which stood in an acre of its own ground, and it also contained another farmhouse.

THE LETTERS
PART IV

1890–1894

Pall Mall & Strutt Street, Manchester, 20 Jan 1890
(Walter Haworth to his sister, Marian)

My dear Polly,

I have just received your letter dated the 14th. So will send you a line in reply right away, to show I am trying to get into business ways. First of all I am glad to hear the children are through the measles alright. Next time you write I hope there will be no return of 'spasms' to report in your own case. You say you are 'as well as usual' does this mean you are not in your usual fighting trim? I trust too that you will soon be able to give better accounts of the 'Master'. Of myself I can give a fairly satisfactory report. My eating is pretty good, and as to sleeping I am myself again, almost. This last weekend I have spent at Eccles with Isaac and his new wife ... George Massey is at my elbow – he says please remember me kindly to Mr and Mrs John – by the way his daughter, Whinney, is now engaged to Lord Byron.

With love to all the children and likewise to John, I remain your affec. brother, Walter

Smedley's, Matlock, Derbyshire July 7th 1890
(Walter Haworth to his sister, Marian)

My dear Polly,

You will promptly recognise (*the*) above heading. I came here on Friday night to report myself to Dr Hunter, and am returning home this afternoon. I am going on quietly but without much change in my condition, if anything gaining a little strength, and happily I continue to sleep well. Dr Hunter recommends 'the saddle cure' so I have to take to riding again. You will, I expect be hearing from Lily about the garden parties at Hilston House: one came off last Thursday and there is to be another one next Thursday. All the rank, youth and beauty of Bowdon have been invited to come and grace the sylvan glades with their prettiest dresses and sweetest smiles. Arthur's young woman was present, of course, last week; though not beautiful, she is, as the Scotchman put it, 'vary intelligent'!

Like my little namesake, you are, it appears, often in trouble. Whatever were you thinking about to be playing with carbolic acid? Sincerely I hope your hand will soon be right again.

I received your letter of the 18th last week and am glad to hear Walter's arm is going on favourably. Now I am going to have a 'physical examination' so, with love to you all, I remain your affct. bro., Walter

Ecclesfield, Bowdon Oct. 1st 1890

My dear May,
I am very pleased to receive your nicely written letter. On the whole I enjoyed my yachting trip, though we had rather too much rain ... Poor Daisy. I am sorry about the two little kittens, but by this time I hope she has been comforted by the love and affection of her twin dolls. By now I expected you would be able to milk more than two cows – you could do that much when I came to see you, and I suppose you are a much bigger and stronger girl now. If Mother can milk four cows don't you think with an effort you could milk her four cows and your two in addition?

I hope Father and Jack enjoyed going to Topeka Fair, and that they bought you something from the fair. Your brother Walter is a very unlucky boy. Tell him to be careful not to break his head, for that is not so easily repaired as a broken arm. Tell Mother I will write to her soon.

With love to you all in which cousin Harriet joins, I am your affectionate Uncle, Walter.

Walter Haworth died on October 30th 1890, and the following note of his death was received:

In loving memory of
Walter Haworth
of Ecclesfield, Bowdon,
who died on
Thursday October 30th 1890
aged 49 years
'Not slothful in business'
'Rejoicing in hope'
'Patient in tribulation'

Emporia, Ks, 19th Nov. 1890
(Marian Haworth to her sister-in-law Marianne Haworth)

My very dear Marianne,
Your letter of Nov 2nd & 3rd reached me yesterday & has been such a comfort to me, the first gleam that has come to me since last Wednesday. After receiving your letter of Oct 28th a week last Sunday, I was terribly anxious. I had been anxious since receiving Abms. first letter, but felt how

the peril had increased, to have to fight through the winter with so much weakness. Walter Varley* went into town both Monday and Tuesday, to see if there were any letters. When he came back without letters, I can't account for it, I said Walter is better or we should have had some word. I became lighter-hearted than I had since receiving Abms first letter, my heart seemed to say 'God has heard your prayers, and has given him back to you all' . Wednesday there was a meeting of the Ladies Society in connection with the church, I said I will go to the meeting, & call for the mail before I go. When I got to the Post Office there were no letters, I waited for the next mail 3hrs. later, I did not go to the meeting. I felt restless for news of him, though not uneasy. I loitered about doing some shopping and waiting. When I went back there was a large bundle of letters. I picked Abms. out and put the others in my satchel, & opened his letter in the office. Can I ever forget the pain of it? I suppose I read every word of the letter, but my mind seemed only to take in three words 'kissing his face'. I only remember the sense of terrible pain, as if a sword had gone into me and a feeling can he be dead? Yes, or why would Abm. say that. After that my mind is a blank, except a sense of despair, until I got to a ford about 1/2 mile from the house, then I remember wondering if the horse would want a drink. I don't think I gave him one – perhaps I drove mechanically or the sagacity of a quiet horse I was driving brought me back safe. I feel as if I could understand in a fuller meaning the word 'stricken' – but I don't want to dwell on my personal loss and desolation. I try to feel he is nearer to me than he was before. The 'narrow stream of death' is narrower than the ocean & I want to be worthy of being his sister. He was always ready to forget himself in care for, & sympathy, & interest in others, the tributes to his memory which I received in Jesse's letter today are very touching & we who knew him most closely, know that there is not a word said about him which is not less than the truth. I wish I could put into words how gratefully and tenderly he spoke of you and Jesse, & Abm. & Bessie and Abm's children when he was over here. He said you all had done more than could have been thought of to make up to him the gap & loneliness caused by Mother's death. Twice when I was in England he said 'whether I get better or not I have had everything that human skill and love could bestow'. Your letter and the copy of Dr Hunter's makes me feel that it is true, everything was done. I had grieved greatly thinking if only he could have been got away before he took the chill perhaps we might have had him for years – probably there was no chill at all – simply a greater exertion telling on the sad weak parts., and instead of grieving I am most thankful that he was not allowed to start, and could have to the very last all the attention and comforts of home and love. Most grateful am I, when I could not reach to help or minister to him, you all made it impossible for anything more to be done. Most reverently and humbly do I use the words 'you did it unto me'. Tell Jesse with my love that I hope to answer his letter in a very few days. Dr Ingalls address is 'President Dr Ingalls, Drury College, Springfield, Mo. U.S.A.' I received Walter's photographs with a wrapper in his handwriting two days after his body was laid to rest in Harpurhey – like you I repeat 'not him only his body', and though the flesh falters the inner self consents and owns God's right to him. I think the verses on his card are beautifully appropriate. I cannot write more – with love to each one of you.

Believe me ever your loving sister, Marian Whitworth.

* Walter Varley was Marian's nephew, the son of her elder sister Harriet and John Varley of Southport

In his Will, drawn up on 22 October 1890, Walter Haworth left John Whitworth £500 'and all sums advanced by me were intended as gifts and nothing is now due to me'. He set up a trust fund of £6,000, the income of which was for his sister, Marian Whitworth, and after her death for her children, to be divided equally between them. His personal estate amounted to £44,987 9s 10d.

By this time John Whitworth must have felt that things were going well enough on the farm that he and his family would stay permanently in America and so on 1st November 1890 he applied for United States Citizenship in the District Court of Lyon County, Kansas, before J.G.Taylor, Clerk. This was eventually granted to him on 28th October 1894 in the District Court of Emporia, presided over by the Honorable W.A. Randolf.

There follows a gap in the correspondence until 1893, but we can reconstruct some of the events in the intervening years. John Whitworth's father, Benjamin, now retired as an MP, suffered a severe attack of illness during 1890, from which he never really recovered. It was at this time that Benjamin and Jane Whitworth, and their unmarried daughters Helena and Bessie moved from 22 Daleham Gardens to 23A Goldhurst Terrace also in Hampstead, London.

On the 7th. May 1892 John Haworth Whitworth was awarded *The Common School Diploma* of School District 71. He had been examined in Reading, Spelling, Writing, Arithmetic, Grammar, Geography, U.S. History and Physiology. The Diploma is signed by Edna Fife, teacher; A. H. Stephens, County Superintendent, Public Instuction; Laura J. Finlay and A.H. Newton, Assistant Examiners.

May Whitworth had been given an autograph book by her cousin Nicholas Martyn Whitworth in 1887, the earliest signature in it is dated

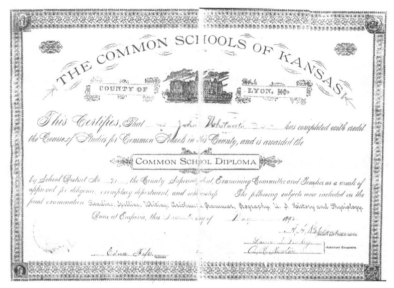

*John Haworth Whitworth's Common School
Diploma of School District 71*

January 15 1892 and is from her teacher, Edna Fife. This is followed on July 10th by Maggie Harker. On November 11th the same year Cousin Goodier Haworth was obviously out from England for a visit. Pearl and Myrtle Eldridge signed it on November 16th they were neighbours (Myrtle Eldridge had taught the children at home in the summer of 1888).

It is possible that at least some of the family visited the 1892/3 World Fair in Chicago. A silver plated spoon inscribed '1492 Chicago 1892/3 World Fair' and depicting Christopher Columbus and the World Fair pavilion must have been acquired by the Whitworth family in Emporia; it has come through the family with the letters via the late Miss Eileen Rogers.

The sudden death, on 5th August 1892, after a serious illness, of their close friend, Dr. Frank Ingalls, President of Drury College, at the age of about 50, must have caused them great sorrow.

Emporia Sept. 28 1893
(John Whitworth to his mother, Jane Whitworth)

My dear Mother,

We were all much shocked to see from the Emporia paper of today that Father was dead. We had been living in hopes that his great natural vitality would have pulled him through. Marian and I had been planning for some time to try to get over to this winter to see you all, and we may yet do so, but Father's absence will be terribly felt. Since hearing of his death I have been living over again the years when we were at Fleetwood and when we were grown up, how thoughtful for our interests Father always was. My great regret has been that misfortune should have struck us all together and that I could not help him out of his financial difficulties, as I have felt for some time trouble and worry were wearing him out. Only a month ago I got such a nice letter from him, he complained of increasing infirmities and difficulty in getting through his work. I do wish we were nearer you that we could comfort you in your great sorrow, we can only pray to God to watch over you and bless and comfort you. What a comfort it is to think that death is only the beginning of a better and fuller life. I enclose you the cutting from today's paper. If his fortune is gone, his reputation for good and noble work still survives. Helena and Bessie will miss him very much. I am sure they have done everything for his comfort during his illness they could think of. Marian has been very ill with the Quinsey, but is now nearly better again. All the children keep well, I am thankful to say. Marian sends her love and sympathy and is sorry she cannot be nearer you in this time of sorrow and trouble.

Your affec. son, John.

Benjamin Whitworth died from blood poisoning, caused by an injury to one of his hands a few weeks previously. He died on Sunday 24th September 1893 in his seventy-seventh year, and was buried in the West Hampstead cemetery.

Emporia Sept 28th 1893
(John Whitworth to his sister Mary Boyd)

My dear Mary,
The news of Father's serious illness has caused us great anxiety, but we still had great hopes that his natural vitality would pull him through, but today's Emporia paper informed us that Father was dead. We shall have to wait some 10 days for particulars. The paragraph is headed 'Philanthropist dead' and reads 'London Sept 27th., Benjamin Whitworth the great manufacturer of Manchester and well-known philanthropist is dead'. I suppose it is in all the American papers. I should like you to send

Benjamin Whitworth MP and his wife Jane

me the notices of the Manchester papers. My mind has been going back all day to the times when we were all together at Fleetwood and Prestwich and thinking how kind and thoughtful he was for our interests. Let us know what Mother and the girls and Aunt Jane will have to live on now Father's directorships fees are over. I cannot help but feel that in spite of Father's advanced age that still he has died before his time, killed by worry and hard work. He has indeed fought a great fight but at great cost. Helena and Bessie will naturally feel his loss most keenly of us all, I feel deeply sorry for them. We are very anxious to hear how poor Mother bears up. How the Whitworths have died off since we left England: William, James, Alfred* and Father. Coming home to meet such blanks will indeed be sad and trying. Marian has been quite ill with a bad attack of Quinsey, but is now gaining strength nicely. We have great thoughts of coming over to see you all this winter, but it is hard to manage, so difficult to find anyone to look after the stock properly in my absence. I suffered greatly from my last visit and dread to experience it again especially as farming looks so much more hopeful than it did.

Best love to James and the children

Your affec. brother, John

* *William died in 1886, Alfred in 1891, and James and Benjamin in 1893.*

Emporia, Kansas 28th Sept 1893
(Marian Whitworth to her sisters-in-law)

My dear Helena and Bessie,
Our thoughts are entirely with you all today and though the Great Ocean divides us we are all bearing our common sorrows and bereavement together. Our hearts and spirits are united not only in grief but in our belief in happy reunion and life hereafter when we shall be able to see the why of so many of life's mysteries.' On earth the broken arcs in Heaven the perfect round' (Browning). We have been very anxious since receiving Mary's letter, but we did most devoutly hope that your dear father might be spared until we could see him again. It made us feel that at whatever cost we must get back to England as soon as possible. Mary's postal of the 16th inst. made us feel hopeless of recovery. I have had a severe attack of quinsey and seemed to have no strength after it had gone; I would almost faint going across a room. There is a lady in town who has been so good; she wanted to take me to her house and nurse me and I could be near the doctor, and since I recovered she kept pressing me to pay her a visit and the change would strengthen me. I did not like to leave John in his anxiety but he urged me to go and said he would bring any letters he received from London. So this morning I drove to town with May and Jack and took them to school, intending to stay in town a few days. I had a good deal of shopping to do. You may imagine my shock. The first store I went into a gentleman asked me if it was John's father whose death had been telegraphed to the daily paper of this town, he then gave me the paper to read. There seemed to be no doubt it must be true so of course I came right back home to try to help John to bear his loss. When I came back he saw me, he said 'Why have you come back, is Father dead?' Poor fellow he is just heartbroken, he sobbed like a child when I told him, and all afternoon and evening he has sat still in his chair thinking, the tears streaming down his face all the time. This has made him feel the distance between us more than anything. I know how it feels, I have been there, and I don't think life will ever take away the bitterness of not being able to be with my Mother and Walter to the very end, and not seeing them to their last resting place. We are very anxious to know how Mother bears up. Can she tell me who wrote 'God's finger touched him and he slept?' It has been running round in my head all day. It seems almost selfish not to be glad that he has gained rest and peace after his brave fight and struggle against adverse circumstances. He has been a grand and good man and I have always been glad to have been connected with him. You girls have his spirit and unselfishness and we have much to be thankful for that you have left nothing undone that could be done for your Father and Mother, but it has

been hard for you to have so much responsibility. John feels so deeply not having been able to help your Father in his difficulties, but the spirit was willing. If we come to England we can talk things over. Give my dear love to Aunt Jane she will feel it hard to lose 4 brothers in so short a time. I often think I would like to write to her, but I really do not have the time or strength.

With much love to you both and deepest sympathy, your loving sister, Marian Whitworth.

14 Brown Street, Manchester Oct 2 1893
(Robert Whitworth to John William Stuart)

My Dear Sir,

I am sure you will excuse my not writing earlier, but I have been very fully engaged lately, this must be my apology. Your kind letter of sympathy with many others which we have received have been very acceptable more especially to his widow who has been laid aside so long with bad health. His daughters have been quite worn out, altho they had a night and day nurse to help them. My brother's health began to break down after a slight attack of paralysis some two or three years ago when at John Brown & Co Ltd Directors meeting, but the immediate cause of death was quite a complication of ailments. He met with an accident to his hand which took bad ways, and blood poisoning set in. When recovering from that then his lungs were affected, and shortly before he died his heart also was kept working with injections of Ether. He was unconscious and very deaf shortly before he departed this life. I also looked up to your dear father as one of the best friends B.Whitworth & Bros had among a very large circle....Our friends have been very forebearing to the old firm ever since 1879 when such a vile deception was played on us by a brother-in-law of my brother Alfred who has also gone, let us hope to a better Home. I am now left the only brother, but two sisters are still living. Remember me kindly to Mrs Stuart, and allow me to wish yourself better health in the coming years.

Yours sincerely,
Robert Whitworth

Benjamin Whitworth, by his Will signed 11th August 1891, left everything to his two unmarried daughters, Helena and Bessie. His effects were valued at £2,554.

Benjamin's widow, Jane Whitworth, John's mother, did not survive her husband for long. She died on 21st January 1894, aged 78, whilst staying at Norwood, Burlington Road, Altrincham, Cheshire, with her sister-in-law, Jane Whitworth. Probate was granted in London to her brother, Joseph Walker, corn merchant. She left £500 to each of her children – John, Jane, Mary, Elizabeth and Helena from a Trust set up for her by her father, Thomas Walker, who died in September 1849.

The Whitworth family from Emporia did return to England in the winter of 1893/4, but it is not clear if they arrived in time to see John's mother before she died. The family was photographed together in the conservatory at Woodside, Bowdon (the home of Marian's brother, Jesse Haworth) on Tuesday 6th February 1894. They were in Bowdon on February 4th when Nellie Clarke (their former nursemaid) and Minnie Thompson signed May Whitworth's autograph book. On February 6th Marianne Haworth (Jesse Haworth's wife) and Bessie Haworth (Abraham Haworth's wife) also signed it.

Their visit to England must have been particularly sad as it brought them face to face with the deaths of their closest relatives: John's parents and Marian's mother and youngest brother. It is believed in the family that Marian never got over the death of her brother, Walter.

The Whitworth family on their visit to England, at Woodside, Bowdon, 6th February 1894

Emporia Kansas 16 April 1894
(Marian Whitworth to her brother Abraham Haworth)

My dear Brother,
It was very delightful to read your letter and feel you and Bessie were having such a sunny visit and I trust the benefit of it will long remain with you. You would hear we had a pleasant passing visit from Mr. Baines. He had not heard from his wife from the time she was with you – he had been travelling s'o fast his letters had been unable to catch him up. The spring is very late. We had a week of summer weather at the beginning of last month, then the cold spell came on which lasted until Saturday.

Yesterday the cherry and plum trees came out suddenly in bridal attire and from a mass of dark stalks are now a mass of snowy whiteness. After our last year's entire failure of fruit, we look anxiously for all signs of a fruitful season. The children are still going to school. They took mid-term examinations and were able to pass, so they are not thrown back by the time they lost at the beginning of term by their visit to England.

30th April
The foregoing was not worth sending, but it shows I had started a letter and intended to answer your beautiful letter, which greatly comforted me. I have had to pass through much suffering, having had a most vicious attack from my old enemy, quinsey, and have come out feeling worsted and prostrated. I began with severe aches and chills, and had a sore throat. We started at once with Dr. Hunter's written instructions and John went off for our doctor. He agreed with the mode of treatment and added some medicine, which he said would throw it off if anything would do it. For several days the quinsey on that side seemed to be kept in abeyance, and to make some slight improvement, and then the old side, the one that has been so troublesome, started in, though all the time these preventions were being used, yet it started in with a vengeance and though the Dr. was coming all the time and trying to give me relief by making openings and letting out matter, still it kept on getting worse until the tonsils met and for 14 hours I could not swallow a drop of medicine or water, and could hardly breathe. I fully realised my life was in danger, there were so many things I would have liked to have arranged. One was I would like both Jack and Daisy to be taken to England to be educated because, from careful study of their characters, if they did not have their mother, they do not seem as naturally adapted to the ways of the country as the other children: but they are very happy dispositions and are not aware of any incongruity. I would not like to leave any wish behind it would be hard or unwise to fulfill; circumstances change so much, I don't feel so strongly

about it as I did. But when I was ill, if I had strength, I believe I would have written you about it. It is possible the question may never have to be considered, but I thought there was no harm in telling you.

4th May

Oh! dear, it does seem as if I never shall get this letter finished. I have felt so tired and faint and unequal even to writing, though I have been thinking of you all the time. I note what you say about keeping the two girls, that was my own idea, and when our old girl came back I made the proposition and said that if they would behave, and do the washing, I would keep them both – but I never had such a time of misery– running to each other all the day, hindering each other in their work, the work never being properly done, the meals never on time, at meal times I had always to go and hurry things up and help to dish the food for the table. I sent Maggie away after a 3 week trial. I would much rather have kept her and sent the one I brought out from England away. She was at the bottom of the mischief, and the other one was weak. I don't know how the Dr's. wife could reconcile her conscience to give such a good character with Amy. She is flighty, flirty, untruthful, passionate in temper. I have no confidence in her, but she is away from her own country, she has no home and does not seem to have any friends. She has only had one letter from her sister since she came, but I must lay low until I am well, then if she doesn't improve, she must find herself another situation and I another girl, and count Amy's passage out as a bad debt.

The children have been so good and affectionate, doing everything for me in my illness, poulticing, steaming etc. The letter, I fear, will sound rather doleful, but I am really much better. Do you remember at St Anne's telling me when people are getting better they must not compare their progress day by day but week by week and sometimes month by month. Each day I don't feel much encouraged, but today, when I think of a week ago, when I could not even sit up in bed without feeling faint and having to lie down, and today I have been lying nearly all day on the Ilkley couch on the S. porch basking in the sunshine and listening to the birds. The couch was worth bringing if only for today's enjoyment. Perhaps a letter from Lily has gone astray. I have not heard from her since about the time you started for the South of France. I had a letter from Marianne at Southport.

With dearest love to you all, Ever your loving sister, Marian.

P.S. I was indeed thankful to hear of Frank joining the church and rejoice with you and Bessie, that you are all members of the household of faith. It makes us long and pray we may have the same joy in our children.

Lovingly yours, Marian.

(Note written on the top of this letter: Copy of our dear Polly's last letter addressed to Abraham and received just a week after the receipt of the cablegram announcing 'Marian died suddenly last night' – that would be May 9th.)

THE EMPORIA DAILY GAZETTE *Thursday May 10th 1894*

DEATH OF MRS JOHN WHITWORTH

Mrs Marian Whitworth, wife of John Whitworth died very suddenly at her home five miles east of town yesterday evening. She had been somewhat indisposed during the day and had her supper sent to her room. She died without any warning whatever while eating the meal. She had been suffering with rheumatic fever, and it is supposed it went to her heart. She was 45 years of age and leaves a husband and five children. She was a native of England and came here about eight years ago. She was an estimable lady and beloved by all who knew her. The funeral will take place tomorrow morning at 11 o'clock from the First Congregational Church. Rev. Pearse Pinch will conduct the service. The interment will be at Maplewood.

She was buried in the Maplewood Cemetery (Block 16 Lot No N 1/2.45) on May 11th 1894 and the inscription on the memorial stone reads:

> *Marian, wife of John Whitworth, born January 14 1848,*
> *died May 10 1894.*
> *'I am the resurrection and the life, whosoever liveth and believeth in me shall never die.'*

Emporia May 24 1894
(John Whitworth to Miss Thompson in Bowdon, England)

Dear Miss Thompson,
   Your letter of May 15th came to hand yesterday and I hasten to thank you and Miss Minnie for your kind words of sympathy. Words can never tell the loneliness I feel or the intense longing to see and speak with her once more. It would have been easier to part with her if she had only been able to bid me goodbye ere she passed away. She had been particularly happy and cheerful all the day she died and I am persuaded had not the slightest idea of dying. I had been in town but got home about 3 o'clock

found she had some fever and complained of a pain in her right knee. I sent Jack for the doctor and he came out at once, and prescribed for her. She chatted to him on a variety of subjects for 20 minutes or so, soon after he left the supper bell rang and I went down. She had her supper taken up and Gladys stayed with her, talking with her all the time, when suddenly she fell back on the pillow dead. Gladys called out 'Father come quick something's wrong with Mother'. I flew upstairs lifted her head but she only breathed once after I reached her, not the slightest movement in her limbs, death must have been instantaneous. We buried her on Friday, over 30 carriages going to the funeral. She was dearly loved by all who came in contact with her and they mourn her as a sister. We are not sorrowing as those without hope, we know the call was 'This day thou shalt be with me in paradise.' It is only for ourselves we are so sad. I know now as never before how closely our heartstrings were interwoven and what a terrible sore was left when they were pulled so rudely apart. The children are very good and comfort me greatly. Oh how they miss her. Thank God her blessed influence still remains, she being dead still speaketh.

Yours very sincerely, John Whitworth.

Hilston House, Altrincham May 25th 1894
(Abraham Haworth to his brother-in-law, John Whitworth)

My dear John,

I recd. on the 17th inst. Marian's note which she began on April 16th & continued it on Apl. 30th & May 4th. It was mournfully interesting to read, & is now specially precious. Your note of the 9th. came yesterday. I now feel that we know all the details we can know. She had a sad experience between the 16th and 30th April. We can never be too thankful that so good a life was given to us for a while; so richly gifted and so gracious in its spirit. She was answering my last letter to her from Cap d'Antibes on March 22nd – I wish you would see if she kept it, & if she did, return it to me or a copy of it – whichever you prefer. We now long to know how you have got on since she died, & what arrangements you contemplate for the future, & hope we may hear from you soon & frequently. A few lines from any of the children to any of us here will be very welcome always. With love to them in which all here heartily join,

I am my dear bro. sincerely yours, Abm. Haworth.

Marian Whitworth died without making a Will. She left an estate as follows. On 31st May 1894 John Whitworth became guardian with L.J. Heritage and J.M. Steele as sureties for $7,700. This sum was made up of an insurance policy with New England Mutual Life Insurance Co. $2,500 and one half interest in three mortgages, and other personal property. She also left the following:

Mortgage note Robert L. Peck	*$500*
Mortgage note Caroline L. Peck and A.J. Peck	*$500*
Mortgage note E.E. Rowland and Lucy M. Rowland	*$500*
Mortgage note Alice Pearson	*$100*
Cash as per bank book May 1/94	*$ 75*
Coupons paid on above Mortgage	*$115.33*
Note Hannah Williams	*$47.60*
	$1,837.93

A detailed account of her funeral expenses also survives; they were as follows:

Lot in cemetery	*$30*
Hearse and horse and B. for Rev Pearse Pinch	*$10*
Digging grave	*$4*
E.B. Peyton Probate dues	*$10.35*
Monument in cemetery	*$150*
Curbing stone round Lot	*$30*
Labour on same	*$17.80*
J.H. Frith retaining fee	*$25*
Undertakers fee	*$72*
Dr Gardiner	*$15*
Cheques signed by M.W. and received by	*$71.40*
bank after her death	*$5*
	$15
	$455.55

On 7th December 1895 John Whitworth, as Guardian, applied to make a loan of $2,600 from the estate of Marian Whitworth. $1,200 at 7% paid every 6 months to Mrs Kosiah Gilbert and Abraham Gilbert; and $1,400 at 7% interest to Ellen O'Toole, a widow, Michael O'Toole unmarried and A.M. O'Toole single.

The final administration documents of Marian Whitworth's estate were signed by Helen Whitworth 5th October 1896.

Emporia June 10th 1894
(John Whitworth to his sister Helena Whitworth)

Dear Helena,

I enclose for your perusal a letter from Tom* received yesterday. If Helen would only come out for six months or if after trying it making up her mind to stay some time, it is hardly worth while going to the expense of having her out here for a short time.

Every day makes it more apparent to me that it is necessary in the children's interest to have a lady at the head of the house. Our hired girl is pretty rough and very little of the lady about her. Everything in the way of eatables, table service etc. is degenerating very fast and May don't seem as yet to have any power of asserting herself, or really very much knowledge of how to go about it. Daisy is a much better housekeeper and Boss than May but of course she is too young for the hired folks to pay any attention to her. I have written to Mrs Jesse explaining the situation, perhaps you had better consult with her as to what is best to be done. I enclose a letter to Helen which you can send on after seeing Mrs Jesse, if you think it wise, in any case you better write to her as she will be expecting a letter. I am sure just the right person is waiting somewhere if only she could be found. They need a thorough Christian lady, kind and sympathetic but where is she to be found? Oh how terribly I feel Marian's loss, as a companion, as adviser, as Housekeeper, yea in a hundred different ways. I am trying my very best but it is hard to be both Mother and Father to a lot of children. I have not been feeling at all well, cannot sleep. Dr. gave me some sleeping medicine but I only took one dose as I dreamt most horribly. I am 10lbs lighter than I was when I got back.

We are having delightful weather and every prospect of an abundant harvest. Jack and May finished their college term yesterday so will get along pretty well for a time.

Your affec. bro. John.

(In case Helen comes out Mr Jesse would advance her passage monies.)

Tom was John and Helena's elder brother and Helen's father.

The summer of 1894 was the driest on record up to that time. Only eight or nine inches of rain fell on a large section of the Great Plains and thousands of farmers experienced complete crop failure (H. Steele Commager 1982, 230).

Emporia, Kansas 24th July 1894
(John Haworth Whitworth aged 15 1/2 to his aunt Mary Boyd)

Dear Aunt Mary,

I know you are wondering why I did not write to you before, but I was so busy that I didn't have time to. We have had no rain here for over a month and the last two or three days we have had great heat and no wind. Today the thermometer was at 105 F in the shade. We have very poor prospects for Indian corn as it is firing at the roots and if it does not rain within two or three days we will have only 5 or 10 (*bushels* ?) an acre instead of 40 or 50. The dust is 2 or 3 inches deep on the road and when driving you can only see 10 or 12 yards in front or behind. We have cut 2 crops of Alfalfa this year. I did the raking and ran the go-devil for half a day. Walter and I have been fishing lately but with little success - the biggest fish we have caught weighed only about 4lbs. We have 5 colts, 8 calves, and 70 lambs this year besides innumerable pigs that wont stand still long enough to be counted. I see that he sky is clouding up and so will close with the hope that it will rain. Give my love to Uncle James and my cousins.

I hope you will write me soon, I am your loving nephew, John Whitworth.

During 1894 McInley (the Governor of Ohio, later President of the United States) visited Kansas City on a campaign tour. He spoke to an enthusiastic crowd outside the railway station. The town was en fete and the school children were given a half holiday to mark the occasion. Suddenly there was an interruption, struck by something McInley said in his speech about tariffs, John Whitworth interjected a question. The audience tried to silence the lad but McInley said 'No, let him speak, his question is intelligent'. John repeated his question about the advisability of increasing the revenue by a tax on imported luxuries. After the meeting McInley came down and shook hands with him and said 'One day you will make a name for yourself'. (Retold in an obituary notice in the Bowden Guardian 1918 by the Rev. Hewlett Johnson M.A., an Oxford friend of his.

This also recounted in William Mackennal's Life of John Whitworth (1918), pp. 38–39.)

Helen Whitworth decided to come out to Emporia to help out her Uncle John and her cousins. It was a brave decision for a young girl who had never before spent a night away from her family in Lancashire.

Pictorial cheques signed by John Whitworth, October 1894

THE LETTERS
PART V

1894–1895

Helen Whitworth c. *1894*

Helen Whitworth was the eldest daughter of Thomas Whitworth and his wife Elizabeth *née* Shaw. She had an elder brother, Arthur, a younger brother, Thomas, and four sisters: Florence, Ethel, Alice and Hilda. She sailed from Liverpool at 4 p.m. on August 15th 1894 as a saloon passenger on the *Britannic*, a White Star Line, Royal and United States Mail Steamer, run by Ismay Imrie and Co. of London and H. Maitland Kersey, New York. This was one of a series of ships which left Liverpool for New York every Wednesday. The Commander was E.J. Smith RNR. Amongst the 219 saloon passengers listed was Mrs Frances Hodgson Burnett, the author of *Little Lord Fauntleroy* (1886), and her maid. They arrived in New York on August 24th.

R.M.S. *Brittannic* 10am 16th August 1894
(Helen Whitworth to her youngest sister, Hilda)

My dear Hilda,

As I have a stamp I will write a few lines to you. My boxes were put in the Doctor's cabin last night till a berth was found for me. I was getting a bag out when I overheard this conversation between the steward and the stewardess. 'Miss Whitworth has to have a berth in 83 tonight and if there is a better one tomorrow she has to have it.' (Steward) 'But she can't change, they have to put a lady passenger from Queenstown in a cabin which has three in.' (Stewardess) 'Well, but orders are from Mr. Ismay and Mr. Hughes that this lady is to be specially looked after.' (Steward) 'Oh, well that alters the case.' I am getting very well looked after, and the two gents Mr. Ashworth introduced me to, speak. Mr. Simpson has 85 cabin, the people in my cabin will have the door open so I saw Mr. S. go off to the bathroom in his dressing gown. I want to go out now so must close. Mrs Hodgson Burnett is a passenger. Don't fret but think that the time has passed and I shall be coming back again. With much love to you all. I am afraid I was cross yesterday when we were all scrambling about on the boat, if we only had stood still we should have found the Purser, as he was looking for us to tell Mother he would look after me.

Goodbye, I am your ever loving sister, Helen.

Bowdon, Emporia, Kansas. Sept. 20th. Sunday afternoon
(Helen Whitworth to her aunt Mary Boyd)

My dear Aunt Mary
I really will get my letter written to you, and Aunt Helena and Aunt Bessie must let it do for you all this time but I have had so much to do ever since I came, I have only had time to write home and if I leave my letter writing till after supper there is so much noise. Mother will most likely have let you know about my journey here. I enjoyed the boat immensely, but the train was most uncomfortable, and it was so hot. I was glad to get to the end. I was sorry to miss seeing Mr. D. Boyd, it was only by a few minutes, Mr. and Mrs. Herron were very nice to me. Unfortunately Mrs. H. was ill all the time, so could go out with me. I left them on Sunday afternoon and got here Tuesday afternoon. Uncle John took me to Mrs Frith's to have a cup of tea before driving out here. It was very mean of Maggie* leaving like she did, but it is just as well as it seems she was very rough and vulgar, she has done Daisy a great deal of harm. She had everything her own way since Aunt died and things were in an awful muddle. I can't find half the children's clothes yet, they scarcely had any underclothes ready for the cold weather, and they must have had things made to go to England with. May is much like Florence but as well as being lazy she is very untidy, her clothes look as if she had slept in them, and she never touches a needle if she can help it, but very few of the American girls can sew nicely, they do everything with the machine and it is not a tidy way. Jack says I am almost as bad as Aunt Mary in making him brush himself, I don't know how he gets so dirty; he had not a single

clean collar, so I set to and got some up. They think it does not matter how they look except when they go to town, it is such a pity they have got into that way.

Gladys is a nice child and is the most even tempered of the lot. She and Jack have gone off in the Buggy to Sunday School about four miles away and they will bring Emily** (our girl) back. We drove her over to her home yesterday as she wanted to go to a teaparty. She is very nice and quiet, rather slow, but I hope she will improve in that respect, she has not had a fair chance yet, and we have so much to do, and I have done as much as I possibly could, but there is a lot of work here. I don't wonder at Aunt Marian getting tired out, especially as she did the bulk of the cooking.

We have had one of the men laid up with typhoid fever, Mr. Faulkner came and helped move him, he recovered sufficiently to get away for a change on Thursday, it was a relief to my mind. I have not been feeling extra grand myself, and have had indi. so badly, but hope to be alright again soon. It has gone cooler today and that will be better. Rain is wanted badly, the rivers and wells are drying up. We had a few thunderstorms three weeks ago but that was not enough, though they certainly made the countryside look a little better, a lot of corn has not been worth cutting this year. I have got to know a few of their friends. We had quite a crowd out here last Sunday afternoon, I like a Miss McDonald and a Miss Kisiah and Mrs Frith the best and when I am in town, which is not often, I go and have a chat with them. The two first have a big milliner's store, it is a paying business. I am afraid they will be leaving at Christmas and going to Kansas City as Miss Kisiah is going to be married and will live there. Aunt Marian always stayed with them when she wanted a little change. We go to town every Sunday, I go to Chapel sometimes and sometimes to Church with Mr. Faulkner. I do not know whether you have heard that he is engaged to Maggie, it seems a pity as he is a gentleman; like Uncle Ben he has not enough to marry on yet.

They have not mentioned lately in my letters from home how Aunt Jane is, so we hope she is improving and you are all keeping well. You will have got quite settled down again after your trip to Windermere, and I am looking out for a letter to tell me all the news. Sometimes I feel such a long way from home and wonder if I can stay the two years. Hilda writes to me very often. I will try not to be so long before writing again. I must close now as I have the milk to see to and it is almost supper time.

With fondest love to you all from your ever loving niece, Helen Whitworth.

Uncle John wants to know if you will ask Miss Betsy what it was she used to make with wheat, milk, flour and nutmeg, he says they used to have it after harvest time, he thinks it was called 'frummerty'*** or something like that and he wants me to make some if you can get the recipe.

*/ 'Maggie' is Margaret O. Harker who married Walter Falconer in May 1895./

**/ Emily Merit, a native of Kansas with some Indian ancestry, aged 22 in the March 1895 census./

***/ He is referring to frumenty, a traditional English dish made from newly harvested wheat grains cooked slowly in milk until the starch grains burst and flavoured with sugar and spices. Sometimes an egg yolk was added at the end of cooking (see Dorothy Hartley:/ Food in England 1954)./

Emporia, Kansas, U.S.A. Tuesday *(late September 1894)*
(Helen Whitworth to her sister, Hilda)

My dear Hilda,

I suppose you will be home again, you are quite coming out in a new light, school is on now isn't it, let me hear how you like it and what you have to do, and please remember me to Miss Richards. Fancy today being Willie Poole's wedding day, I laugh when I think of it, it is a good thing I burnt his letters before I came away. Tell Florence I was glad to hear from her, & hope she will write again after she has been to Fleetwood. Girls are considered old maids here after they get to 23, so I am on the shelf now. People are so curious I am amused at the remarks I hear. I am getting quite a dab hand at getting up early and seeing the sun rise. I hope Mary and Annie don't require so much calling. The people here dust their rooms once a month on average, think that sweeping is quite sufficient. Looking through one of the cupboards I found a sweeper so have mended it up. The beds are quite different to ours & they put the pillows on last. My bed is very comfortable, now I have got used to it, it is a spring mattress. Who helps Ethel to make the beds at home? I generally make them here. May helps on Saturday and Sunday. Church is quite fashionable, it begins at 11 a.m. & 8p.m. the service is never longer than an hour & a quarter. How was it Charlie Ashton did not go to Sephton with the others, I am surprised. Tennis seems to be over early. I shan't get much here, the swells play it in town but that is rather a long way to go. I have only been away five weeks, it seems a lot longer does not it; the *Britannic* will be back in New York directly. Did you see her when she was in last time?

Nobody says how Mrs Gates enjoyed her trip to Ireland. The winter card playing seems to be starting early. We play Halma and Draughts but you see we go to bed at 9.00 or ten so have not much of an evening. Whatever made Mrs Bradshaw call, I am surprised. I hope Florence and Ethel had a good view of the Duke and Duchess.

How did they get on with the Bells, you seem to be having quite a procession of visitors again. I am glad Willie Whitworth is looking better again & hope he will keep alright. I have not read the Waterloo Times yet. Tell Florence to get me one sent every Saturday. I heard from Mrs. Herron last week, her little boy has had measles, so I just missed it nicely. She says that if I ever feel homesick I must go and stop there for a bit, but if I get that far I should want to come all the way home. I should like to go and see Dora sometime and there are cheap trips to Texas. Now I must go to bed, if I think of any more I will add it in the morning. The stamp on the envelope is for father, is he still doing as much of it as usual? I hope you are well and Grandma keeps pretty fair. This is a very stale letter but I don't think it would interest you to hear about the horses & cows & sheep & pigs, & there are heaps of those, Uncle John does not know how many he has himself. Then there are 5 cats and 5 dogs, one is an awful thief. We were having chicken for dinner today & it ran off with them & so we had to catch and kill some more. You would laugh if you saw me going about with my yellow sun bonnet on. People here take great care of their complexions. My burnt hand is getting better, though it looks red, yet it has been very bad.

With much love from your loving sister, Helen.

Bowdon, Emporia Oct 28th 1894
(Helen Whitworth to her Aunt Helena Whitworth)
(Thanks for the *British Weekly*)

My dear Aunt Helena

Thanks for all your letters I am so pleased to hear from you and to know how you are all getting on. We are all pretty well here first one then another gets a cold but not serious, and I don't wonder at anyone catching a cold it is such a changeable climate. We have had it quite as hot as summer till this morning and today it is a case of winter coats. It looked likely for rain this morning so Uncle John thought we had better not go to church so only he and Walter have gone. I have just finished straightening up the house and the children and seen that dinner is going on alright and am now taking this opportunity to get some of my home letters written. If I leave it till afternoon somebody is nearly sure to call, and in the evening

Helen Whitworth's parents, Elizabeth and Thomas Whitworth,
and her sisters, Florence, Ethel and Hilda

we always have music. I am getting quite settled here, and now the weeks don't seem so long. I can assure you there is very little time to feel homesick, night is the only time, when I can't sleep. Uncle John looks better than he did when I came. I don't think he will ever go home again to live, he seems to have made up his mind to stay here,* and has been getting a little more land. This farm is decidedly the best round here; of course the farm yards and that part are not kept so straight as English ones but here Uncle John has only two men to help him, and in England would want five or six. We manage to send eggs and a little butter to town every week, the butter is really splendid, we are getting 7 1/2 cents per lb. for it and they think that a good price, and we sell a little of the best Jersey milk and get a penny a quart for that. I have been very busy cleaning the house, the carpets all wanted taking up, and the blankets and curtains had not been washed this year, so Emily and I have been getting all done; we only have the kitchen and pantry left now and are leaving them until the flies get a little less troublesome. Then the dressmaker was out for three days and we got better dresses made for the girls. I got them a very nice black serge, the bodices have a little ribbon on them and they look very pretty. They have all got good jackets and hats. Do you remember the button off Daisy's jacket, it was still off when I got here. They are the most untidy lot. I am trying to get them a little better, but it is hard work. Emily fortunately takes an interest in them and if I am not about when they are going to school she watches them. I am glad we have such a nice girl. I don't know how long after Christmas she will stay. I hope into the spring at any rate. She is not very strong so I have to help her a good deal in the mornings. I wrote so far and then it cleared up a little, Gladys and I thought we would go for a walk. (I don't get enough exercise out of doors, no-one goes walking here, and I go on very rare occasions to town). It was dinner time when we got back and directly after Gladys, Daisy, Emily and I went to Sunday School at Plumb Creek, 4 miles away.** School was nearly over but they have a service after and today they had a good minister out from town, so it was very nice. It is the first time I have been out there, some of them go every week. Both the Congregational and Church of England ministers and their wives have called on me, and some of the people, they all seem very kind, everybody thought so much of Aunt Marian. We see very little of Mr. Faulkner, I don't know if he is mad over Maggie leaving and seeing that we can get on very well without her. She wanted to come back again. I was in town yesterday and saw her for the first time, I did not care for the looks of her. I wonder if she will ever marry Mr. Faulkner, he is getting to look very old and worn. I am sorry Uncle Ben*** is so unsettled. Uncle John thinks he should come out here.

Griggs, Watson, & Day, Printers, Davenport, Iowa.

UNITED STATES OF AMERICA,

STATE OF KANSAS, Lyon County, ss:

BE IT REMEMBERED, That at a term of the District Court, holden in and for said County, in the City of *Emporia* therein, on the *28th* day of *October* in the year of our Lord one thousand eight hundred and *Ninety four* was present the Honorable *N. A. Randolph* sole presiding Judge of said Court, when the following among other proceedings were had, to-wit:

John Whitworth

a native of *England* and at present residing within said state, appeared in open Court, and makes application to be admitted to become a CITIZEN OF THE UNITED STATES, and it appearing to the satisfaction of the Court that he had declared on oath before *J. S. Traylor, a Clerk of the District Court in and for Lyon County, Kansas, on the 1st. day of November, A.D. 1890,*

(a Court of Record, having common law jurisdiction, and using a seal), two years at least before his admission, that it was BONA FIDE his intention to become a CITIZEN OF THE UNITED STATES, and to renounce forever all allegiance to any foreign Prince, Potentate, State, or Sovereignty whatsoever, and particularly to *The Queen of Great Britain* of whom he was heretofore a *subject* and said applicant having declared on oath, before this Court, that he will support the Constitution of the United States, and that he doth absolutely and entirely renounce and abjure all allegiance and fidelity to every foreign Prince, Potentate, State, or Sovereignty whatsoever, and particularly to *The Queen of Great Britain* of whom he was a *subject*

The Court being satisfied that said applicant has resided within the United States for the term of five years next preceding his admission, without being at any time during the said five years out of the territory of the United States, and within this state one year at least; and it further appearing to the satisfaction of this Court that during that time he has behaved as a man of good moral character, attached to the principles of the Constitution of the United States, and well disposed to the good order and happiness of the same. Thereupon the Court admitted the said applicant to become a CITIZEN OF THE UNITED STATES, and ordered all the proceedings aforesaid to be entered of record, which was accordingly done by the Judge of this Court.

IN TESTIMONY WHEREOF, I, *M. Q. Starr,* Clerk of the Court aforesaid, have hereto set my hand and affixed the seal of the said Court, at office in the City of *Emporia* in said County, this the *29th,* day of *October* in the year of our Lord one thousand eight hundred and *Ninety four.*

M. Q. Starr, Clerk.

By *A. P. Buck,* Deputy.

John Whitworth's Certificate of American Citizenship, 28th October 1894

I do wish he was settled in something good, it is so hard on him and Florrie. I hope they are both better than they were when I left England.

It must be very trying for you and Aunt Bessie being with (*Great*) Aunt Jane so much, you have had so many years of being with sick people. If only I was at home I could help you a little. It is funny to think that we are as far away from New York as you are. Mrs Herron asked me to go to stay with her next year for a little while, but I said if I get to New York I should want to go home. I dare say that you have heard that Mabel Hardy has come to New York to try and work up a private nursing practice. I hope she will be successful. Ethel Hollinger told me, she is very good to write to me every fortnight.

We have a little fox terrier puppy we are trying to teach a few tricks. I am afraid it will never be as clever as Sprite as its teachers do not have the patience of Uncle Ben ...

I don't think I should like farm life for ever, the work never seems to be done, at any rate till 7.30 at night. We shall not be so busy now through the winter, it is so much nicer now we have got rid of the men. It made so much more cooking, fortunately we shall not have more than one again as Bill has got his wife out. They arrived a fortnight ago. It took them four days from New York so I must have been very fortunate. May and Jack will not board in town till after Christmas, if the weather keeps decent. I have tried to persuade May to see a doctor, but she wont. However she has begun to be a little poorly and I hope in a few months she will be better. The three younger ones go to the County School but I don't see that they do much good there. They teach in such a funny way here they only teach them writing, reading, arithmetic and grammar, and Daisy is learning a little United States geography; and they forget most of what they have learned during the summer as the holidays are from March to September, of course it is too hot in the summer. Next year, all being well, they will all go into the town. Please excuse the mistakes as Uncle John is reading aloud and it has been rather distracting. Thank Aunt Mary for her letter, I will answer it sometime. I seem to have so many to write, and I can't get the others to. They say they can't find anything to write about. This letter hasn't got anything very interesting in.

With very much love to you all, remember me to all the relations,
Yours affectionately, Helen Whitworth.

---

* John Whitworth was granted U.S. Citizenship on 29 October 1894, a process which he had begun by applying to the District Court of Lyon County, Kansas, on 1st November 1890. He bought land in the S.E. Quarter of the S.E. Quarter of Section 8, Township 19 from C.S. Cross for

$1,185. The transaction was completed on 10th December 1894: he paid $500 down and the rest to be paid within 2 years at 7% interest.

** Plumb Creek Sunday School was held in S.D. 73 some five miles east of the Whitworth farm.

*** Benjamin Whitworth was John Whitworth's youngest brother.

November 13th 1894
(Helen Whitworth to her sister Hilda)

My dear Hilda

Indeed I do not find a sameness in your letters and hope you will continue writing to me and tell me all the news ... I did not get any letters on my birthday, they all came before. I read *Thelma* in the train coming here, I bought it on the way, and thought it very good. We made a lot of toffee on the 5th November and pulled it and made it into such nice twists. I shall have to show you how when I come home.... . Last Sunday morning we had a big baby in the shape of a Jersey calf lying in front of the kitchen stove. It had been born in the night and was almost dead from cold. We had to give it brandy and hot milk, we never thought it would live but are very glad it did. Uncle John stopped at home to look after it. Last week they found a colt dead. We think it got into the sugar cane and had eaten too much. They have been shooting some of the squirrels as they got to be so many. They are nicer to eat than rabbit so we had quite a variety of meat lately after living on chicken for a week, as we have had sheep, pigs, wild duck, rabbits and squirrels.

On Sunday I went again to Sunday School, a Quaker lady preached and she gave a good sermon. She spoke for over an hour but it did not seem long. My word it was cold driving home. Driving over the prairie is rather like going over the sandhills, it is about the same colour and all ups and downs. After you get 30 miles to the west they have no trees at all, they only grow along the river-side here. It is so amusing, all the people here think I am Uncle John's sister. May and Jack are always getting asked how their aunt likes America. Not very flattering to me is it? I don't think much of the American gentlemen I have seen as yet. I may be hard to please. I hope to go to town one day this week and get some of my return calls paid. I am getting worse than Mother, but it is such a bother getting into town unless I go in early with the others, but I must make up my mind. We have a good many people out, but now they will be scarce for a few months while it is cold. Everybody is very nice and I have had plenty of invitations to stay the night, and that is what I intend to do. Walter wants me to read to him so I will close.

With much love to you from your loving sister, Helen.

I do wish you were here to sleep with me, the hot water bottle is not half so nice as you. The knitting looks so nice on my nightgown H.W.

After the children went to bed Emily, Uncle John and I sat over the fire popping corn, and now I am going to bed. I hate leaving the fire and have been keeping very late hours lately, I made myself some tea last night. Thanks for the papers received today and now goodnight Hilda and everybody.

Box 1144 Emporia, Ka. U.S.A. Sunday night *(Nov/Dec 1894)*
(Helen Whitworth to her sister, Hilda)

My dear Hilda,

You are an angel writing to me so often and sending me the paper. You all must write often as I seem to get home letters every week. I am so pleased to get them. I am sorry I have not much news to tell you but one week is much like another week here. We are going to make plum puddings next week. I have had such trouble getting sultana raisins but Uncle John managed it yesterday. What sort of Christmas do you expect to have, at any rate it will be gaier than ours. I don't know yet whether Miss McDonald and Miss Kisiah will come to dinner on Christmas Day, they always have done. I am so sorry you and Ethel are not so well, hope you are better again & that the others are alright. How did Ethel and Tom enjoy the tennis dance, & how does Tom look in his dress clothes. I shan't know him by the time I get back. Sometimes two years seems a long time to be away and yet the weeks go so quickly, it seems to come round Sunday directly. I always think of you when I am in church, you will be having tea. We got to town so early this morning I got in for part of the Sunday School. The church is such a little one and now they have two big stoves, we go in and stand round and have a gossip and get warm before the service commences. The people are very nice and kind to me. I am not particularly struck with the young men perhaps I have not met the nice ones. I don't think there are very many, they are mostly the sort they call tough, in this part. We don't see much of Mr. Falconer, he comes occasionally and is always very kind to me, he always takes the papers after we have read them.

How did the dramatic go off. I laughed at the order you were going. What is Charley Cottrell like, it seems funny to think of him being a doctor.

Mother and you all seem to have been disappointed in Miss Gates' singing, she always talked as if she had quite a strong voice.

I am glad that Mother's dressmaking has turned out successful. I want her to cut me a pattern someday, if she can by sending my measurements. With all the work I do I don't get any thinner so this place suits me. Tell Mother I have not too much to do at present, the summer is the busy time but the children will be home and they help a good deal. Mondays and Tuesdays are our busiest days. You would have laughed at me yesterday. I was churning and the cork flew out of the churn and the cream flew all over me and right across the kitchen floor I could not stop the thing until it had gone round three or four times.

Is Mr. Besso coming to Waterloo for Xmas. I will write to him sometime but I daresay he sees some of my letters. Mother must have had quite a time when she went to Urmston, she saw plenty of people. How is Ethel Ashworth, does she write you as funny letters as ever? Ethel Hollinger writes to me every fortnight. How is Dr. Simpson he is a funny little man isn't he. I think I shall have to ask him if he can't give me a sort of certificate as a good nurse. I wish I had got something of the sort. Then if I wanted a little extra cash I could go out for a bit. There is not one professional nurse in town, only one creature of the older type and people pay her $8 to $10 a week because they can't get anyone else.

Are any of you going to Colne for New Year? I hope Grandmama and Uncle Robert are keeping well. Arthur seems to be very busy over the bazaar.

I have another letter to write and it is getting late. I hope my next letter will be a little more interesting. I wish you all a very Happy Xmas and let us hope the year 1895 will bring better luck with it. It seems to me that the Whitworth family are getting left on the shelf, the way all our friends are popping off, every letter you write tells of somebody.

Give my love to all with heaps for yourself, Believe me, your loving sister, Helen.

Box 1144 Emporia, Kansas, U.S.A. Jan 5th 1895
(Helen Whitworth to her aunt Bessie Whitworth)

My dear Aunt Bessie

I have been a long time writing to you but it is not that you are forgotten, we speak of you all every day. You and Aunt Helena have had a

State Normal College, Emporia

very sad time* but I do hope that you will both be able to rest and get stronger again. I hope 1895 will not be such a sad year for us, as 1894 was, so many things seem to have happened in it. I was glad when the holidays were over. We made Christmas as cheerful as possible and I think the children enjoyed themselves. Uncle John and I had a day of buying presents, and they all hung up their stockings. They are getting on very nicely at school though they don't like their teacher. I hope Uncle John will be able to send them to town school next winter. The awkward part is who would stay with him here as there would have to be a house in town.

We have had a very cold spell. I nearly froze. The fur cloak and that white hood came in very useful, thanks so much for giving them to me, and the thick vests are lovely. The children all kept well except Jack who was sick one day. I have been in the house for a few days with a bad cold and throat. My throat is better but my cold has not gone yet. I had to go out this afternoon as the man is very ill with bronchial pneumonia and his wife sent to know if I could suggest anything to relieve his breathing. She was up all last night and will be again, but would not let me stay with her as I expect to be nurse tomorrow while she gets a rest. We have had the children here today, Daisy and Gladys have been very good amusing them. There isn't a good nurse in town. Uncle John and I both think that if Aunt Marian could have had one she might still be alive now. He is very worried over Bill and then it makes him so busy as Jack is only home Saturday. We leave them in town after church on Sundays. The Plumb Creek Sunday School closed last week till April. Uncle John preached there a fortnight ago. I was sorry I could not get to hear him.

Mr. Falconer is to be married this month, so Mr. Blakely said when he was down here on Thursday evening. He has been renting one of Uncle

William Faulkmer and Amy Simpson in Emporia

John's farms but leaves it then and Emily's (our nice girl) father has taken it. I hope then as her folks will be near, she will decide to stay with us. She has been so nice this week and done all she could for me. Mr. Blakely has bought a house near here, I hope he will do well on it.

Amy,** the girl they brought out is a great swell. She was visiting the Normal College the other day. I think people are treated too much as equals here, I would rather have our English way, though perhaps we do err too much the other way. There are a good many Welsh people in Emporia but very few English. When Miss McDonald and Miss Kisiah leave, next month, we shan't know an English lady. I like the Congregational minister more every time I see him and his wife is very kind. She wanted me to go to their house last Sunday to get warm. She always speaks to us.

The people Jack and May board with in town look after them well, the only thing is they give them boiled beef for dinner nearly every day and they get rather tired of it.

We are getting quite lazy, don't come down to breakfast till 7 a.m., it is 8 a.m. before we can get all the children down. They take after Father and Uncle Ben and like bed best in the mornings. I will write to Aunt Mary in a few days, will you give her my love and thanks for the books, calendar and letter received last Sunday.

Please write soon and tell me all you are doing and if you have some new work.

With much love to you and Aunt Helena, believe me,

Yours lovingly, Helen Whitworth.

* with the death of her Great Aunt Jane, Benjamin Whitworth's sister on 9th December 1894, aged 83.

** Amy Simpson, sometimes called Emma in the letters, whose carelessness caused the fire which burnt the house down in 1887; she left abruptly in March 1888, and returned briefly in the spring of 1894 before Marian Whitworth's death.

The Census return for 1st. March 1895 give details of John Whitworth's farm. He then owned 590 acres, of which 290 were under cultivation. The water sources for the farm are described as streams and a well 25 feet deep with a windmill used for lifting the water. His 590 acres were fenced, with only 10 rods of hedging. the farm was valued at $8,840 with $100 worth of implements. The cultivated land was sown with 5 acres of winter rye; and of the spring-sown crops 80 acres were under maize, 10 acres under oats, 1 acre Irish potatoes, 8 acres sorghum for sugar and syrup, 10 acres Kaffir corn, and 30 acres of alfalfa. He also had 120 apple trees, 5 pear trees, 10 peach trees, 5 plum trees, and 20 cherry trees. He also had 2 acres of vineyards. In addition he had 40 acres of fenced prairie, and in 1894 had harvested 20 tons of prairie hay. His garden produce was worth $15, poultry products $50, and 250 lbs of butter were made in the preceding year. At the time of the census he had 36 horses on the farm, 9 milk cows, 56 cattle, 100 sheep and 33 pigs. In the previous year 3 horses had died of disease, as had 1 cow and 1 pig. The value of the animals slaughtered or sold in 1894/5 was $300. There were also 3 dogs on the farm. The residents were John Whitworth aged 49, Helen aged 24, Mary aged 16, John aged 14, Cecily aged 12, Walter aged 10 and Gladys aged 8, and also Emily Merit aged 22, born in Kansas. All the children were at school.

Box 1144, Emporia, Kansas U.S.A. *(no date)*
(Helen Whitworth to her sister Hilda)

My dearest Hilda,

Thanks awfully for two letters and the numerous papers you keep sending me… I am very busy now getting the children's' summer clothes ready. I have made Daisy all new underclothes, hers have got too small. All her dresses want lengthening 4 inches. Daisy is making me a quilt, she can sew nicely and she is very good at helping, and is so anxious to learn everything so as to be able to do things properly. I feel so sorry for them without a Mother; it would be dreadful without ours wouldn't it? Please thank Mother for her long letter and the needles, there was 10 cents duty to pay on it, but as they took our bag today, as the office is closed on Sundays, we got it without paying. The needles look the same sort but I have not examined them closely. I hope the treacle jar arrived safely. Do you understand the working of it? When you have enough treacle on your plate just drop the lid, it is ever so much easier than turning a spoon round and round. I wish I could have sent something nicer, but postage is so dear, I must wait until someone is going over. Wait patiently and I will send you something. Will you thank Mother for the dress pattern, I will let her know later how it fits, she must be quite professional at it.

What a nuisance Duster is tearing the curtains. I should keep her downstairs ...

(The rest of this letter is missing)

Post Office, Emporia, Ka. U.S.A. April *(probably May)* 4th 1895
(Helen Whitworth to her sister Hilda)

My dearest Hilda,
Thanks for your nice letter from Urmston. What's going to happen, you going off by yourself. Where is Mr. Besso going to live next, he hasn't written to me for ages & it is his turn. Gladys is writing to you at present, she asked if she could, she is such a nice little thing, I am sure you would like her. You must all have had a fine time on Easter Monday. It made me feel quite envious when I read all your letters. I often thought of you and wondered if you were all together. I was busy ironing all afternoon. I was glad Betsy was well enough to be with you. I am getting quite excited over Fred wondering who will be the favoured one. It is just a year since I was introduced to him at the Literary.

We had a cattle puncher, otherwise a cowboy, here for the night on Sunday. He came to take 35 of our steers out west for the summer. I can tell you we do have some funny folks.

Last week Peggie shied at some dust and tipped May and Jack out of the cart but fortunately did not hurt them much. Sunday School is progressing alright, tomorrow a Quakeress is going to preach. I have heard her before & she speaks very well. Last Sunday was so hot we had to bring our fans out. I bought a plain black one as I think it looks nice for church.

When I get home you will find me awful lazy. If I can ride anywhere I wont walk, there is something in the air here which tires one so quickly. Two miles here seems as far as four at home.

Tennis will soon be over for the summer, they commence playing as soon as the frost goes & then play again in the Fall right up to Christmas. Are you going to play this summer?

My shoes have all cracked up. I tried all over town for some furniture polish but they all told me nobody polishes furniture, but whenever it got dull just put another coat of varnish on, so I had to make some polish at home.

I had a letter from Aunt Helena on Tuesday & she sent me the pattern for the knitted doyley, it is funny where my book went to.

I have not done much reading lately except the papers. We like the novelettes you send very much. I bought a hammock today so you can think of me being in it reading these hot summer afternoons.

The knitted edging you gave me does very nicely. Daisy is crocheting me some for an apron now & she has just finished piecing a quilt for me of blue and white calico.

I had a long letter from Mrs. Herron the other day and was surprised to hear they were not going home this summer. I suppose Gerty will stay on, they were very busy removing to another flat.

The churches were very nicely decorated for Easter - all in apple blossom & different fruit blossoms. All the spring flowers seem to be purple, at home they are mostly yellow. The lilac is all over & the wisteria by my bedroom window is in flower. I wish you were all here & then I could easily feel at home, & we could have such a good time in the timber & on the hills (a little larger than the sandhills). The mosquitoes are rather a bother by the river, but they don't bother us very much up at the house. Kansas used to be a big inland sea – we can find shells along the creek banks. Gladys brought in a pocket full yesterday, some are quite pretty.

I have not any news this time. You see if I tell you much about the local news it would not be interesting as you do not know the people. One thing I must tell you. I am called an old maid – I am sure I don't look as old as most American girls of 19.

I pity you having the Amersleys making such a row, they want choking.

With much love from Helen.

Emporia, Kansas May 4th.
(Gladys Whitworth to her cousin Hilda Whitworth)

My dear Hilda,

As cousin Helen is writing I thought I would write too. We have a donkey, his name is Edward. Daisy, May, Emily and I had a tea party this afternoon. Our school has been out five weeks. We have 49 chickens, Emily and Daisy feed them. Cousin Helen bought a hammock. Walter and Jack have been fishing today. Cousin Helen and I are going fishing someday. We have a horse sick and a cow sick. We have about 85 lambs. Daisy has a pet lamb. It follows her about the place and she has learnt it to drink. We did not have a shower in April. There will be a lot of fruit if we have rain.

Your cousin Gladys Whitworth.

On May 17th 1895 John Whitworth bought 80 acres of land which adjoined that which he had purchased from Returah Kirkpatrick in June 1889. It was the south half of the S.E. Quarter of Section Four in Township 19. He bought it from Alfred and Esther Abrahams for the sum of $800.

Post Office, Emporia, Kansas U.S.A. May 31st 1895
(Helen Whitworth to her aunt Jane Bryning, née Whitworth)

My dear Aunt Janie,

If you don't often hear from me it isn't because I don't often think of you, but because I always seem to have a letter from 'The Alton'* or 'Norwood'** to answer and somehow I seem to have more letters to write than I have time to write them in. In the winter evenings I felt cold, in fact for some weeks the ink used to be frozen solid if it was further away from the fire than the mantelpiece. Now we have it very warm, it is pleasant enough after supper when our numerous duties are done and we can sit on the verandah and gossip. I bought myself a hammock and hang it by the front door, then Uncle John sits on the step and the children come all around. It is the pleasantest hour of the day, our talk generally gets round to the home folks.

Yesterday was Decoration Day, when everybody goes to the cemetery to put flowers on the graves. It was originally just for soldiers, but everybody has taken it up. Uncle J., the four girls and I went yesterday with flowers for Aunt Marian, everything looked very nice. Has Aunt Mary received the photo Uncle J. sent a few weeks ago? We think it better enlarged than the original in the group.

May and Jack's holiday commences after next week, and they wont be sorry, they are feeling a bit fagged out studying for the exams. The others have been having holidays these last two months.

Till last week the outlook for farmers was most depressing, everything was burnt and dried up. Since then we have had three nice showers which just saved the corn. Most of the first crop of Alfalfa hay was got in last week. Haymaking is not so much trouble as at home, it dries so quickly. It is a good thing there are three or four crops a year, it is the best paying thing on the farm. We pay for our groceries in butter and eggs: butter has been very cheap since November, it has only twice been above 6 1/2 cents and that for the best.

We must be as quiet here as you are, the winter seems awful, only a stray farmer or two, it has to be very nice before our town friends venture out. They are terribly afraid of rain in these parts, they are not used to it like we are, but half the folks own umbrellas, mine has only been out twice in nine months. Social affairs are few and far between so we prize those we get. Last Friday evening we were invited to a Strawberry supper and (my usual luck) it rained, so that was off. On Wednesday the Episcopal Church had arranged a picnic in the timber and we intended having a good time and it rained again. Gladys was most disappointed, she had made her donkey and cart look so nice ready to take the children for drives. Uncle J. gave it them this spring. We can let them go off by themselves and know they are quite safe. Daisy is going to town tomorrow to stay at Mrs Frith's and Gracie Frith is coming out here. She and Gladys are great friends and like the country best, and Daisy likes the town. I think the change will do her good as she has not been quite so well lately. Both she and Gladys are growing fast. I have had such a time this spring lengthening and altering all their clothes. May's clothes fit Daisy very well. Walter will be the smallest of the family, he seems quite strong now and full of mischief.

I hope that you are feeling stronger now. We were sorry to hear in every letter that Aunt Janie is not well. I wish you could come out here for a trip. I feel quite settled, it seems more than nine months since I left home, and I should like to see them all. The life was so strange at first I thought I never would get used to it. The part I disliked most was having the servants always with us. The two men we had last autumn were horrid, but we have a nice quiet one now and Emily is more like a lady's help would be. She is a splendid girl for getting up, is downstairs soon after five every morning and we are having breakfast soon after six. Unfortunately she is not strong and consequently I have more work to do. We both keep pretty busy all day. Daisy is a splendid helper and always ready to do anything for us.

We have been busy this week canning and preserving gooseberries. For the last three years there haven't been any peaches, but this season the trees are loaded. Fruit will be plentiful if we escape the hailstorms. Emporia is quite a nice little town, the big schools make it more lively.

There are 1,600 students at the State Normal and a good many others at the other three schools.

The Congregational Church seems to be the fashionable one. The Americans dress too elaborately for church to suit my taste. I go one Sunday to the Episcopal and the next to the Congregational every other Sunday I stay at home to cook dinner. I have got so far on with my cooking that I am not afraid of spoiling it now. Our Sunday School is doing very well. The last two Sundays the room has been full.

Mr. Falconer was married to Maggie three weeks ago. I thought I had better be polite so Jack took me to call on them and they returned the call last Sunday. It is very late and I must be off to bed, all the others have been gone for hours, they are wise but I don't see much use going to bed early as I can't sleep till late on.

Uncle John joins me in much love,

Believe me your ever loving niece, Helen Whitworth.

* The Alton, Bowdon was the home of Mary and James Boyd, her uncle and aunt

** Norwood, Altrincham, was the home of Jane Whitworth, another of her aunts.

Emporia U.S.A. June 2nd 1895
(Helen Whitworth to her sister, Hilda)

My dearest Hilda,

I have just been reading over again your nice long letter of May 15th. I am sorry you wont get such a nice one back from me, but my doings can't be very interesting. I felt rather seedy this afternoon so did not go to Sunday School, but had a good time out in the hammock and read the novelette you sent me yesterday, they are so nice to read as they are so easy to hold. After I read it I fell asleep and dreamt I was at home, I could not make out where I was when I woke up.

Ethel would be awfully scared if she lived here by the lightening we have almost every night, and it is so brilliant, I like watching it. Last Thursday was Memorial Day, or the day they put flowers and flags on the soldiers' graves, one gets so sick of all the old soldiers, they make such a fuss of them. Now nearly everybody takes flowers to put on their friends' graves. We took a basket full but it was so windy, so would soon be spoilt. There are not many wild flowers here in spring, later on there are more when the sunflowers come out, they are a nuisance they grow everywhere, we can't keep the garden path clear of them, they are 30 or 40 times bigger than the marigolds in our back garden. Our flower seeds have not done at all well, it was too dry. Who is looking after the garden at home? The radishes have grown so big since the rain, they are fatter than a breakfast cup & 6 or 7 inches long.

Daisy went to stay with Mrs Frith for a week or two and Gracie Frith* came out to stay with Gladys, those two have fine times together. Tomorrow they are going out in the donkey cart for the day wild gooseberry picking. Gladys had a lovely white kitten given her yesterday... We are having lots of your sort of dinners now it is hot weather, we always have coffee and now that meat does not keep very well we have to use ham and eggs, and eggs and ham. We shall soon have plenty of fruit. I am looking forward to the water melons etc. the eating cherries are almost over. Daisy and Gladys have commenced having music lessons, but they don't get on half as well as you did. You must be getting on well. I don't do much practising, I play a few waltzes and that sort of thing... What a long time it seems since I was at home, just a year ago I was thinking of coming out. Robert Scholes, Ethel and I walked to Sephton Church... Fancy Ethel being 22 yesterday it makes me look horrid old doesn't it. You will have to keep young and wear short frocks for a long time. I was in town yesterday and had tea with Mrs Frith, the heat and wind made my head ache so I retired to bed early and will go early tonight as tomorrow is beastly washing day. Emily does all the washing and I fold the clothes, we have all done generally by four. Tuesday morning we iron; there are plenty of blouses and frocks now. I like having my crepon one washed for it does not require ironing and always looks and feels nice and cool. I hope to have a more interesting letter for you next time. I enclose a puzzle for you to find out... I will send the answer next time.

With very fondest love from your loving sister, Helen.

* *Gracie Frith later married Ernest Ballweg; he died in 1935, and then she opened a tea-room first at 518 West Fifteenth Street and then at 927 State Street in Emporia.*

Tree Puzzle (newspaper cutting taken from The Advance, *a church newspaper)*

Social tree	Pear
Dancing tree	Hop
Tree nearest the sea	Beech
Dandiest tree	Spruce
Kissable tree	Tulip
Tree where ships may be	Bay

Tell-tale tree	Peach
Traitor's tree	Judas
Tree which is warmest clad	Fir
Languishing tree	Pine
Chronologist's tree	Date
Tree which makes one sad	Weeping Willow
Aspiring tree	Ivy
Industrious tree	Broom
Tree which never stands still	Caper
Unhealthiest tree	Sycamore
Egyptian Plague tree	Locust
Tree you see down the hill	Plane
Meddlesome tree	Medlar
Yielding tree	India Rubber
Tree which bore a curse	Fig
Reddish-brown tree	Chestnut
Reddish-blue tree	Lilac
Tree like an Irish nurse	Honeysuckle
Venerable tree	Elder
Builder's tree	Woodbine
Tree in your hand	Palm
Getting up tree	Rose
Very smooth tree	Satin
Tree which is not me	Yew
Steersman's tree	(H)elm
Fisherman's tree	Basswood
Schoolmaster's tree	Birch
Trembling tree	Aspen
Tree to which all aspire	Pop(u)lar.

'No doubt with a little thought you will be able to add several more to this enigmatic list of trees; and one might get up some very pretty things with the names of flowers.' Phoebe Bird.

Emporia, Kansas June 29th 1895
(Helen Whitworth to her sister, Hilda)

My dearest Hilda,

I received the two lots of papers last Tuesday, also your last letter so now I have two to answer. Indeed your letters are not stale and I love to get them. I send you this time the answer to the Tree Puzzle, those marked we could not answer, and I did not think them good. I did not put them on your list. They were in a Sunday paper and they made a nice S. evening amusement. I have not read many books lately but am going to begin *Trilby** next week. The family Heralds and papers take most of my spare time. Our Ice-Cream party went off very well. We had heaps of ice cream and cake; we hope to have more this summer. Next Thursday is the great 4th. July, all except Daisy, Uncle J. and I have arranged to go off for the day. I think I would just as well spend it at home and have a quiet time. It is the one great holiday in the year. I hope it will be fine for the people. Last Sunday week there was a cyclone 10 miles away from here. A lot of damage was done and some people killed. We were afraid the cloud was making for here. It looked like a big funnel and we thought it was a waterspout, the children were picking cherries but got called in. Being on a hill we could see it quite plainly and saw it drop. You asked me what I do in the afternoons. I generally try to sleep for an hour, if the flies will let me and if it is not too hot, then I read and sew and have afternoon tea, and go down the garden for fruit and vegetables, and sometimes help Gladys look for eggs, and after supper we sit on the porch and gossip. I wish you could see our porch it runs on two sides of the house and it is completely covered with virginia creeper and morning glory, it is so shady and there always seem to be a breeze there. We used to tie the Frith baby up in the hammock and it would sleep there for hours... Gladys has such a nice white kitten and it is a splendid mouser. It always sits on Uncle John's shoulder at nights. Then we have four dogs and three wild canaries which have to be fed a dozen times a day. They have grown quite tame and sit on our fingers to be fed. We had a little squirrel but the kitten killed it yesterday.

From all accounts I shouldn't think the Shahzada was worth waiting to see, I expect the tea was the best part of the trip to Liverpool. Has Mr. Besso been over lately, when you see him tell him he owes me a letter, please send his new address & then I will write to him.

You must be all turning out great swells in your new clothes. My chief thought when I am in Church is how soon can I be home & get into a loose wrapper. I went to Sunday School in one last Sunday as I was too lazy to put my dress on again. I don't know whether I told you I made myself a sunhat out of tea matting and calico. I cut it by the wash basin in my room so you can tell the size. I don't think I shall get sunstroke when I have it on. I have just finished reading the papers you sent me, I am glad Tom is doing so well at cricket, I should like to watch a game. It seems so funny to have nowhere to go at nights except round the farm. Last Sunday evening we found a horse in the pasture with its legs broken, it had to be killed. We have been most unfortunate in our horses. Uncle J. has been breaking two more in: it is so interesting watching and they quieten down so quickly. The W. as they call it is an excellent invention. When are you going to answer Gladys' letter? She talks so much about you and always likes me to read yours aloud. It is her birthday on 27th July we shall have a little party for her... I want to get a pattern for those pretty turn down collars and cuffs, some day when I am in town I will get a fashion book and then write for one. No more room this week so will close now with much love to all from your ever loving sister, Helen.

Thanks for the cream receipt. I made one and it turned out very good.

* novel by George du Maurier, published 1895

Far Creek, Kansas July 12th 1895
(Helen Whitworth to her sister Hilda)

My dearest Hilda,

I am writing you this time again as it is your birthday. I have a little bag for you but I left it behind, so will send it to you later and now send you very best wishes for a happy day, and wish I could be with you and then we could have a picnic at Hightown. Since my last letter all sorts of things have happened. We had very dull but hot weather up to the 3rd. July and thunder every day. On the 3rd. it cleared up and May and I went into town and had tea with Mrs. Frith and we nearly melted. The 4th. was an awful day. All except Uncle J., Daisy and I went off for a picnic, I don't know what they felt like, but we nearly melted. I got as few clothes on as possible and did nothing. At night big clouds rolled up, rain commenced at 12 and in five hours 5 inches of rain fell and the river had risen enough to overflow the banks in some places. We did not think much of it till Friday night, we were wading in the timber and noticed it was still coming up. On Saturday morning it was washing over the hay field 30 feet above the river and the main road to town was flooded in six places. Uncle J. went to town on horseback and had to swim the horse coming back, but he brought me my letters safely. We could not get to the church so spent the morning putting sticks in the water. The weather looked threatening and we were afraid of another downpour, but it was nothing worse than thunder and lightning. The flood turned about noon and left the timber thick in mud, it has spoilt it for some weeks. All our stone wird(?) was washed away, & we had corded enough for ten years, but were more fortunate than our next neighbours as very little of our corn was hurt, & half his potatoes & corn were 10 feet under water. We were badly in need of rain but got a little too much at once.

131

We left home on Wednesday morning about 9a.m. and camped for the night a few miles from Williamsburg. We made friends with the farmer near, he has a splendid farm and a nice house. He invited us to go back that way and stay the night at the farm. Wouldn't his wife feel pleased if we did, it reminded me so of Father. We expect to be away 10 days, and shall look a dirty crew when we get home again, as one gets so crumpled up knocking about all the time. We have some decent clothes for Sundays and will turn out swells then. I am much amused at present watching a party of negroes who are having a day out fishing, and they seem as much taken up with watching us. They do know how to enjoy themselves. The boys have just brought up 6 fish as a start and Gladys is cleaning them for supper. At nights May, Gladys and I sleep in our end and the others sleep in the other, we can divide the wagon in the middle. Two of us sleep on the floor and Gladys sleeps in a hammock. Daisy and Emily are keeping house and making jam etc. We expect to be home on Saturday week and shall feel jolly dirty by then, I guess. I hope to find a big pile of letters awaiting me …

I am sorry to hear that Grandma is not so well. It is quite time mother went to see her again, she does not get very often.

I will write again as soon as we get back, it is awkward writing in pencil.

Give my love to all, and with very much love to yourself from your ever loving sister, Helen.

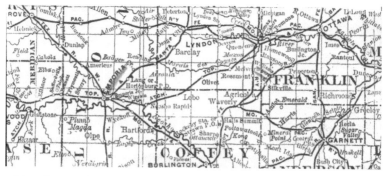

Map showing location of Williamsburg, about 37 miles east of Emporia

THE LETTERS
PART VI

October 1895–April 1896

418, Exchange Street, Emporia, Kansas U.S.A. *(late October 1895)*
(Helen Whitworth to her sister)

My dear Hilda,

I am enclosing a few lines to you in Mother's, and this is private. I will now tell you why. Gertie Fraser is going home on the '*Campagnia*' and I have sent a few little things by her for you all and I want you to go someday to Hightown and get them, and then you can give the little presents as a surprise, they are not what I would have liked to send, but I only had one day to get them in so only had time to make one or two things myself. They are in the white and the black packet. I want you to choose the one you like best, and then send the other to Ethel Hollinger. Dear Hilda please put down all you spend on me and then I will square up when I have a chance. Perhaps May will go to England next spring and then I will send some cash to pay up my debts. I did not know what to get for Arthur and Father, but asked Mrs Herron to put the stamps which were on the parcel inside and those will do for him. Thanks so much for writing me such lovely letters, yours are far more interesting than mine must be, and you send me so many papers. I read the novelette *When Friendship Ends* last night, while waiting for May and Jack to come in from a concert. I thought it a very good one. I have not had many books from the library lately, as I have been too busy sewing. I am getting quite a stylish milliner since Miss McDonald gave me some lessons. I have trimmed new ones for Daisy and May and made my old one look swell. Miss Husband is coming on Thursday to help me make Daisy and Gladys's best dresses, then I shall have all finished except a few little things for myself. I may go out to the farm on Sunday for a week, I think it will be lovely, only Uncle John, the man and myself, and as half the rooms are shut up I shouldn't have too much to do and mean to have a lazy time and perhaps make some Christmas presents, it costs so much to buy things ready made. We are having very changeable weather just now, one day hot another cold. Today we have winter dresses on and fires, yesterday we had all the windows open we were so hot. This is a very short letter but I will do better next time.

With fondest love from your ever loving sister, Helen.

I thought of you often on my birthday. Daisy gave me a pin cushion, May a work case, Jack and Gladys fancy hairpins. Alice Frith made me a pretty pair of garters.

The house at 418 Exchange Street, photos – Professor Robin Higham

418, Exchange Street, Emporia, Kansas. *(Oct/Nov 1895)*
(Helen Whitworth to her sister)

My dear Hilda,

I must write you a few lines to thank you for the pretty veil, it is a most acceptable gift, as I hadn't one without a tear in it I am going to wear it tomorrow for church. I have spent part of this afternoon trimming up my old felt hat (the crinkled one), it looks grand now, and everyone will think it new as I haven't worn it this winter, so I expect to be a smash tomorrow. Many thanks for M.S. (*Modern Society*) and the novelettes came in one post and the newspapers next, your letter explained the two lots.

Please give the enclosed to Mother, I am sorry she is not well and hope the hot water cure will help her recovery, but keep your eye on Alice. I am

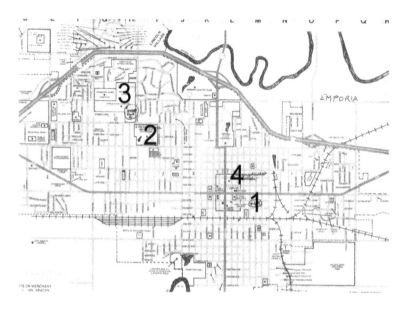

Street plan of Emporia showing (1) 418 Exchange Street; (2) State Normal College; (3) Maplewood Cemetery; (4) Congregational Church

now anxious to hear how Florence enjoyed her dance. I thought of her and Ethel that evening. When are you going to dances? I am sure all the evening dresses must be pretty.

How are the new servants doing, I hope they will suit. I should not wonder if ours leaves when we get back to the farm, as she will have been mistress for so long and will not like having to take a back seat: it is not in the Americans to do it at any time.

No more room this time, with very much love, dear Hilda, from Helen.

418, Exchange Street, Emporia, Kansas U.S.A. Nov. 2nd. 1895
(Helen Whitworth to her aunts Helena and Bessie Whitworth)

My dear Aunts,

I feel very ashamed of myself for leaving your welcome letters so long unanswered. My only excuse is every moment of the day I seem to have been busy. I know if you could be with me for a week you would quite understand. I used to have Sunday evenings but now the Christian Endeavour or Evening Service takes that time up. We have got quite settled in our little town house, and I think I shall find it nice and warm in

136

winter. They do build houses funnily here, we have to go through my bedroom to get from one sitting room to another, and all the first floor rooms have doors opening on to the porch. The first three weeks in September were terribly hot and one Sunday morning it suddenly turned to frost, consequently we all got chills and a touch of Malaria. I have had a bad cold and seem as if I cannot get rid of it. The weather is so changeable at present, 8 and 9 degrees of frost one day and the next up to 60 degrees.

I am writing this out at the farm. I came out here last Sunday for a week and Emily went in to town. I felt I should like a few days quiet and I wanted to get some flannel nightshirts made, and the big sewing machine is here. I managed to get the housework, baking and churning done in the mornings and as I don't muddle up the kitchen I soon got dinner washed up and then had a long afternoon for sewing, and the evening for chats with Uncle John. We have a nice hired man at present, and as he goes to bed early is not much in the way. He is the first one we've had who has offered to carry in wood for me. Gladys came out yesterday afternoon, she misses the farm life the most. They all have settled to school very well. I am so glad they are going to good ones. I am rather anxious as typhoid and diptheria are rather bad, but hope they will escape. We are taking all possible precautions. Uncle John and Emily always spend Sunday with us and in winter will try to spend one night a week.

We have quite a lot of callers, mostly ladies from the Congregational church, the worst is that now I have all the calls to return. The people have not quite fixed up my relationship right. The other afternoon May and I were at an 'At Home' and I was her sister, aunt, cousin and friend.

At present I am getting winter clothes ready. I have finished all the dresses and hats and have just a few petticoats to finish. It's a good thing my clothes don't want much doing to. I only get to look at my fancy work. I did manage to make two little pockets. I sent one to Hilda (Gertie Fraser was returning home last Saturday so I took the opportunity of sending a small parcel). I will tell Hilda to let you see it as they are quickly done, and might sell now the season for evening dress is coming on. I made one in white silk and it looked lovely. It requires 1/2 yard of wide ribbon and 1 yard narrow. My hands are not in condition for fancy work. For the last nine months I have had cracks on the joints and the ends of my fingers, some days as many as seven cracks on one finger, and they are so painful. It is a kind of Excema. I have seen the doctor about it, he does good for a little while but they are soon as bad as ever. He says my skin is naturally very dry and the climate is too dry for it. Having to have my hands so much in water does not improve it. I wrap them at night in cloths soaked in buttermilk, and Mother sent some oiled silk last week to make gloves.

<u>Sunday afternoon</u>

I did not get my letter finished last night, so have just time before supper. Uncle John and Emily have gone *(back to the farm)*. People cannot understand our having two houses. Fancy Alice* is now 21 and Helen Boyd, it makes me feel quite old. Thanks for all your good wishes for my birthday, I had a nice one, though it was spent mostly in the kitchen as Mrs Frith came and helped me make tomato pickles. I must now wish Aunt Bessie Many Happy Returns, my wishes will arrive rather late, but better late than never.

We are so glad to hear about Uncle Ben and Florrie** (have I to call her aunt? it would seem very funny). We were very surprised to hear of their marriage, but I am so glad, Uncle Ben must have been so lonely in his lodgings. When you write again you might send me Uncle Ben's address so I can write to him. I am hungering for a sight of you all and the feeling gets stronger every month. Letters are very nice but they don't make up for a nice chat. We rather think that Mrs Jesse may be vexed because May would not go to Miss Griffiths.*** May and all the children seem to have taken such a dislike to her, it would be no use sending them to be unhappy. I often try to get Uncle John to say he would like to go back to England and have a farm. I must say his farm looks very pretty now and I am sure he would find it hard to leave it. Jack looks much better now with his new teeth and I hope in time his lip will grow straight. The children have grown so much: May is quite as tall as me, and Uncle John's clothes wont fit Jack. Walter is the small one of the family and he seems to have made a start now.

I hope Aunt Martha**** will find a companion. I should not want to be the one. Please remember me to all the relations, tell Miss Bridget I will answer her letter some day...

May and I went to an 'At Home' the other day, they are by no means such stiff affairs as those in England, we quite enjoyed ourselves and met some nice people. Miss McDonald wanted me to go and spend a few days with her in Kansas City last month, but I could not leave the children while they are at school, so I shall try and get there for a few days when the Xmas holidays are on, a little change freshens one up so much.

With very much love to you all in which all join, believe me your ever loving niece, Helen.

I hope you will be able to read this, my pen finger is the bad one today.

Uncle John hopes to hear from Uncle James soon. H.W.

---

* *Her sister, and Helen Boyd was their cousin, daughter of James and Mary Boyd.*

138

** *Uncle Benjamin was the youngest child of Benjamin and Jane Whitworth. He was born in 1862; in 1895 he married Florence Elizabeth Lovell, and they had one child, Benjamin, born in 1896.*

*** *see the first letter (21 July 1884) when May was at Miss Griffiths' school at Saltaire*

**** *Martha Whitworth, née Walker, widow of Robert Whitworth (d.1895) and younger sister of Jane Whitworth (d. 1894) the wife of Benjamin Whitworth, (Helen's grandmother). Robert Whitworth was a younger brother of Benjamin Whitworth M.P., and began his business career in the firm Benjamin Whitworth and Brothers, cotton importers and manufacturers. He was an ardent advocate of the temperance movement, liberal in politics and a member of the Manchester Reform Club. He was also a great supporter of lifeboats. They lived at Oversley Cottage, West Road, Bowdon.*

Exchange Street, Emporia, Kansas U.S.A. 16th Nov. 1895
(Helen Whitworth to her sister Hilda)

My dear Hilda,

I am sure it must be your turn to hear from me. I was so pleased to get your letter of 29th. Oct. You will by now have seen Gertie Fraser. Mrs Herron wrote me that one parcel had been smashed in the post. I hope to hear soon that the contents were not much damaged. What do you think of the milkweed balls? I mean to try to make some extra nice balls next summer to bring home with me. Oh, wont it be delightful to see each other again, and what a lot we shall have to tell each other. Since I last wrote nothing special has happened till this afternoon, when just before Uncle John started for home, the horses ran away, they had not gone more than 300 yards when they banged into a tree, smashed the pole, and turned the Surrey over. Uncle John had the pleasure of riding home on one horse barebacked and leading the other. It was the young horse that got scared. I am sorry as they wont be safe for May and I to drive for some time to come.

I saw in the paper last Friday that there had been a big storm on the 11th in England, I hope it was not as destructive as the last one, when so many boats were lost.

This past week has been lovely, slight frosts at nights, but quite hot during the day, and able to keep doors and windows open. The week before was horrible, every day wet and mud almost too deep to go out. Uncle John could not get into town for some days. Thank goodness that it is exceptional weather or Kansas would not be fit to live in. I never saw so much mud and the rooms get so dirty, not having any lobbies to come into.

We have all our stoves fixed for winter at present. I let them just smoulder all the time, put a little coal on morning and evening and shut all the draughts and then they require very little attention and yet are always ready for the sudden changes that always occur here.

I did not go out today till after supper, then May and I went to the C.E. at the

Emporia postcard: the Post Office

Congregational. I gave my name as a member, as I think I may as well get to know some of the younger people. After the C.E. we went to the Episcopal. The first time I have been to Evening Service since I left home. It seemed quite nice. I rather like what I have seen of the new minister. St. Mary's church seems to be quite getting to the front, there is always plenty about it in the *Waterloo Times*. I do like getting the papers from home. How do the Gates' like their new house, is it larger than the one they left? This house is a cozy little place, the kitchen is especially nice and bright. I was ironing there on Wednesday afternoon when the little girl (about 7 years old) from next door came rushing in and got hold of me saying, oh, do come quick our baby is dead. You may be sure I dropped my iron and ran and found the baby in convulsions. It did not take me long to rush back for hot water and I was getting its clothes undone when the lady from the other side came to my assistance, and we were just getting it round when it's mother arrived, and very glad we were to see her. Her husband is a doctor and he came in for a little while, so I came off. Mrs. Webster has never called on us, though we are such near neighbours, perhaps she will now. I went into nearly all the rooms looking for things, it was so funny.

Emporia postcards. Above: City Library; Below: Commercial Avenue

Now I must answer a few of your questions. My hands are much better just now, of course kitchen work does not improve their looks. So you have called your kitten Moses; we have a lovely cat called Snowball and four more of various colours, then we have six fox terriers. We have only one kitten in town with us. I have not been reading any interesting books lately, they don't seem to have many new ones in the library, and what they do get are mainly American. I read a rather nice one by 'Pansy' the other Sunday called '*New Graft*'.

Who is Florrie Smith that you all keep talking about. You mention a new name so often I get kind of mixed.

Now I must say good night, dear, With very much love from Helen.

141

418, Exchange Street, Emporia, Kansas 23 November 1895 Sunday night.

(Helen Whitworth to Hilda)

My dearest Hilda,

I will send a little letter to you in Ethel's.* I hope you have received your bag by now, though I'm afraid it would be sadly crushed. I thank you for all the papers etc. that you send me. I would send you an Emporia paper but don't think it would interest you. I put one away intending to send it with an account of the cyclone, only six miles away from us: three churches and 12 houses were blown away. I dare say our roof would have gone if we had not had it strengthened last year.

Tonight at church a little brown dog came and sat in our pew and growled and barked during most of the service. I felt mad as I was afraid the people would think it belonged to us. I suppose harvest festivals will be commencing now. They don't have such things here, and they could decorate the churches so nicely, with the varieties of corn they have... I hope Mary's foot is getting alright, it must have made it very awkward for you all, it gets sort of monotonous washing dishes, doesn't it? Now there are only the 6 of us to wash for we soon seem to get done, and somehow I can cook without dirtying a big pile & messing the kitchen up. You would think this house very funny. The front door opens into the dining room and you go through it to the kitchen, and another door in the dining room leads into my bedroom. In my room one door leads out onto the back porch, and another into the sitting room. In the sitting room one door opens onto the staircase, and another on the front porch. If you want to go from the sitting room to the dining room without going through my bedroom we have to go out onto the porch. The kitchen has a door opening outside, and the cellar steps are close to it, and the well is about 2 yards from the house. It is very deep and seems to take such a long time to pull the bucket up, but the water is lovely and cold, just like ice. The railway is a block away, the trains make more noise than ours as they have to ring a big bell while going through the town, then the whistle on most of them is like a steam fog horn.

Does Mr. Phillips still take *Modern Society*, if so you might ask him if he will let you have it to send to me occasionally. Miss McDonald used to give it me and Mrs Frith, but now she has left we have to do without it, and we like scandal sometimes.

I have been reading *Mr. Barnes of New York* again, it takes so long to get a new book from the library. I go there and read all the monthly papers, it is quite a cosy little place. Now I must off to bed, I hope you are keeping well, I expect letters this week from some of you.

With very much love to all and heaps to yourself from your loving sister, Helen.

* *Ethel was their sister.*

418 Exchange Street, Emporia. Dec. 10th 1895
(Helen Whitworth to her sister Hilda)

My dearest Hilda,

Yours was the very first letter I read this afternoon, and the news it contained* upset me very much. It was good of you all to write to me. I should like to be at home with you all, it seems so long to get news. I was just finishing reading my letters when two ladies appeared at the door, I thought once of getting under the table and letting them think I was away from home, but they saw me through the glass. My eyes were all red, you know how one looks when they are crying, but I had to invite them in. They were two ladies from the Congregational Church set. I met them at the Chicken Pie Supper. I have sent Tom** by this mail my photograph, I had it taken as a Christmas Card and everyone says it is pretty good. If I have any left over I will send you one, but some are printed too pale and make me look as if I was ill. I thought I would have it taken in my new blouse, it has come out very well. I have got no new things this winter, black dresses keep tidy longer than other ones and we have been in mourning so much lately. One Miss Whitworth engaged is the only bright spot in the year 1895. How I shall hate going to Colne the first time again, it will feel so changed. I think it much the best that Alice's*** engagement should be made public, people talk so much. I am glad that Mother told Uncle Robert... The scented bag was for Alice, but I also sent about 30 balls of various colours and sizes for you others, they must have tumbled out between here and New York. I will make some bags for you all next year, all being well.

Now, dear, I must close, I hope Ethel's neuralgia is better. I shan't send Xmas cards. I couldn't very well wish you a Merry Christmas, but trust you will all spend a happy day, and think of me sometimes as I shall often think of you. I will write again next week.

With very much love to all especially to yourself from your loving sister, Helen.

* *These letters told her of the death of her grandmother, Ann Shaw, née England, (1811–1895). She was the daughter of Abraham England, corn miller of Broughton (between Skipton and Colne) and she married Robert*

Shaw J.P. of Colne Hall, cotton manufacturer (1809–1885). Their daughter, Elizabeth, married Thomas Whitworth – the parents of Helen. Elizabeth Whitworth, née Shaw, had two brothers, Robert and Thomas, and a sister, Eleanor.

** Tom was Helen's younger brother.

*** Alice was Helen's sister who married John Marsh of Liverpool.

418 Exchange Street, Emporia, Kansas Jan. 5th. 1896
(Helen Whitworth to her sister Hilda)

My darling Hilda,

I received your letter of the 24th. yesterday, and the papers today, thank you so much for all. You can't imagine how much I look forward to mail day, and whatever I am doing has to wait when the postman comes. I have just come in from church, there are special services being held this week, and as it was nice I thought I would go.

I got back from Kansas City last Friday, just in time for dinner. I had a delightful visit and was very sorry when the time came to say Goodbye to Mollie (Miss McDonald) and Pem (Miss Kisiah). The weather was lovely all the time, very cold the last two days, but I did not notice it, everywhere was kept warm, even the street cars had stoves in. I left here on the 27th. Dec. Gladys went to the station with me and saw me off. I was five hours getting to Kansas City as two engines broke down. I felt so sorry to think of Mollie having to wait so long for me at K.C. station, such a wretched hole. It did not take long to get up to Hotel Cordova where they board, the diningroom closes at 7.30 but they kindly waited for us and gave us a good dinner. We then went upstairs (by lift) to our rooms and commenced to make ourselves look beautiful, as there was going to be a small dance for people in the hotel and their friends. I was glad of the opportunity of seeing how Western Americans dance, and when they commenced I laughed so much Pem said she would turn me out of the room, but she was just as bad herself. The first dance was a Waltz, they went so fast and worked their arms up and down just like a pump handle, I know I could not do it and so declined to make a fool of myself. I danced four round dances later on with two Englishmen, and managed to get through two sets of Lancers with the Yankees. There are only three figures to the Lancers and they were not a bit like ours, but I managed to get to the side and watch what the top did. One very pretty dance was called 'The Oxford', then there were plenty of gallops, polkas etc. There was also some very good claret punch which I enjoyed. At 12.30 we had luncheon (as they call it in these parts), sandwiches coffee etc. and the negro waiters danced a breakdown for us. We retired to bed at 1.30, I felt rather tired as I had been up since 5.30. Next morning Mollie got up early, but was kind enough to send Pem and me breakfast in bed. It was delightful to feel I had nothing to do but be lazy. We got down to the store by 10 a.m. and I spent the day very happily watching hats get trimmed and going round the store trying various ones on, and looking at other people buying them. In the intervals we did plenty of talking, as not having seen each other for nearly a year we had plenty to say. At 6 o'clock Mollie made Pem and me go up to the hotel for dinner, she stayed at the store as they do not close for dinner till 10p.m. After a very good dinner Pem and I went to the theatre to see '*Trilby*', I like the play immensely and it made it nicer having read the book. It is a funny story isn't it? I was quite a swell (instead of taking their hats off in the stalls they wear very fancy ones) so I had on a Paris pattern one, cost £5, it suited me splendidly.

On Sunday morning we all had our breakfast upstairs and just managed to get to the Cathedral as Mass commenced. After Mass we went out to one of the suburbs on the cable cars for a ride, the cars go so quickly and Kansas City is so hilly, it felt rather like being on a switchback. In the afternoon we ate chocolates and went to sleep. In the evening we called on an English family called Watkins and Leibstatern (Jews), they were having a card party, but soon gave up playing and we had a good tuck in on oysters and brown bread.

Monday I had a look round the city and in the evening some friends came in and we had cards. Tuesday we were busy in the store all day. After dinner we had music and later on went into Mr. and Mrs. Deans' rooms and stayed with them to see the New Year in. I know you would think of me as I thought of you all, and we drank the health of all at home. You must have felt quite a small family at home this Christmas. I am sure Mr. Besso would be disappointed. We had a quiet day, but very nice. I went to see Mrs. Frith after mailing my letters, brought Gracie and Alice back with me for supper and afterwards we played games till 10 o'clock. I did not get many cards at Xmas but more have come these last few days... I hope Tom got the photo. I would send you one, but the two I had got crushed in the box. I was very pleased to get all your Xmas cards, I haven't heard from Florence lately, but hope she will write from Colne ... Are the Marshs' a large family – Alice mentions two or more aunts, cousins etc. every letter. I am getting quite bewildered amongst them all.

Next time I go to the post office I will try to get the stamps father wants. I hope Mother is keeping well, she must have so much to do &

think of just now that you must take extra care of her. With very much love from your loving sister, Helen.

(no address, no date but clearly January 1896)
(Helen Whitworth to her sister Hilda)

My dear Hilda,

I will send you a few lines this time, I unfortunately lost my letter list, so can't remember whose turn it is, but will answer Alice's letter next time. You always write don't you. I always look forward to your letters, that was a splendid one I received ten days ago. I am glad you think the photo a good one, and am sorry I have not another one to give you, but the only one left got crushed in my box, and does not look better for it, so I hope that Tom will let you look at his whenever you want.

You must have had warmer weather at Xmas time than we had, for though it was cold we had plenty of sun. Till last Wed. we had it dull and many wet days out of the 10 then it changed to blizzard and we are now having it very cold. The snow keeps clean and crisp and it is nice to walk on.

Yes, thanks, we are all very well except that yesterday morning I ran a knitting needle into the back of my hand and it has made my hand feel very painful and swollen. I keep putting poultices on it so hope it will soon be alright again.

Aunt Mary sent us a six months' volume of *Strand Magazine*. I think it is quite as good as it used to be.

Alice seems to be having a fine time, she has rather changed. Do you remember how she would never see anyone, and would cry if we made her? There is a little girl goes past here every morning who reminds me so much of Alice in the old ulster.

I hope your teeth have stopped aching. I went to the dentist a few days ago and had four filled, and have two more to be done sometime. Like you I had to retire to bed with a bad headache last Monday but was alright again next morning. It was such a warm day even my jacket felt heavy, so I put it all down to the weather.

I am a member of the C.E. at the Congregational Church and we got the cards for the 1st 6 months last Sunday. I was rather startled to see my name down on the Missionary Society, and in turning over the page was still more so at seeing my name down to lead a C.E. meeting on April 5th. Fortunately they give us a topic to talk about and I have some time to think about it.

I was much obliged for the novelettes. I read them in the morning while I was watching the dinner. Our next door neighbours are trying to be friendly. I went to a teaparty with Mrs. Webster last Wednesday, and the other night I went to keep house for her and while I was there the Dr. came home and we had a little talk, he told me he was born in Tredegar.* No more room, so goodbye, with very much love from Helen.

Tredegar, S. Wales was where Helen Whitworth's grandfather, Benjamin Whitworth M.P., had had interests in the Tredegar Coal and Iron Co. and played an important part in turning it into a limited liablity company.

418 Exchange Street, Emporia, Kansas. January 25th 1896
(Helen Whitworth to her Aunt Helena Whitworth)

My dear Aunt Helena,
I wondered if the scrap of paper I put inside Uncle John's letter would reach you. I received the parcel of texts yesterday so know that it did. The texts are very pretty and I thank you for getting them for me. I tried here, but they could not understand why I was not satisfied with some already coloured. The children are very anxious to begin and paint them. Mother has some money of mine, so if you will tell her what I owe you she will pay the debt.

Yesterday was the end of term, both at the Normal and the City Schools. All the children have done very well this time and the three youngest will pass to a higher grade on Monday when the new term commences. I hope they will work hard and be as successful at the end of the next twenty weeks. Gladys was not well when I wrote to Aunt Mary, but she is quite well again and very lively. Daisy had to write on a piece of paper what she intended to do when she had finished school (the question was one they have to answer at the end of term). I happened to see them and Daisy had written 'Father's housekeeper' . She will make a good one, as she is so anxious to learn how to do everything properly. We are having winter weather at last but must not grumble after having had such a mild winter. More like an English winter. Snow looks lovely here and keeps so white, walking is rather a difficult task at present, the paths have such a thick coating of ice.

Everything is decidedly slow at present, there are no lectures or anything on, next month the Normal Course will commence again and it is always pleasant going there.

The Congregational Church is still without a minister, so we have to wander around each Sunday. Last week they gave a Mr. Wagner a call but he had already accepted another offer, so the committee was disappointed. We did not care very much for him. I am a member of Christian Endeavour,

May generally goes with me to the meetings on Sunday evenings. It will be my turn to lead before long and my topic is 'The Gift of Life and how to use it'.

I have been taking a little holiday from sewing since Christmas, only doing mending, but shall have to start again next month. When I do have much machine work to do I go out to the farm for a few days where I have more time, though Emily says she is overworked. Do you know if the Haworths have thought of anyone else to take my place? I feel I must go home to see them all this year, though if no better arrangement could be made I would come out again for another year or 18 months. I am very fond of the children, but Jack has been very trying these last few months and makes it very uncomfortable for me at times. When Uncle John is here he is alright. I am afraid I am too near his age to have proper authority over him and yet have to keep telling him about things for as you will remember he is not particularly neat. Walter is improving wonderfully and very tidy.

I commenced china-painting last week as I thought I might as well have a few lessons as the knowledge may come in useful one day. I pay 2/6d. a lesson for a lesson about three and a half hours. China is expensive, it all has to be imported.*

I was not at all surprised at Uncle Robert's Will, my only wonder was that I got £100 as I did not expect anything. Arthur seems to find it a difficult job to find a suitable house, Ethel, I suppose will have to be housekeeper.**

I have been fortunate in finding many kind friends here, some of Aunt Marian's and some new ones. Aunt Marian was loved by all who met her and people are kind to me because I am her niece.

Uncle John was in to dinner today but as it is cold wont come to church tomorrow, but he promised to come and stay all night sometime during the week. He is looking very well but finds it very lonely at the farm and wont be sorry when we all get there again. I suppose that will be the first week in June. When I go out we have quite a nice time together and such cosy evenings in front of the big fire, surrounded by numerous dogs and cats.

With our united love to Aunt Bessie and yourself, Believe me, your ever loving niece, Helen Whitworth.

She painted a set of five tea-plates with a floral pattern, each had different flowers but all were in the same soft colours. No wonder the plates were expensive – they were Limoges china imported from France. I still have them.

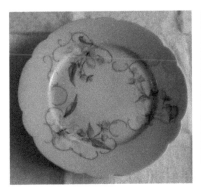
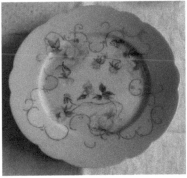

*** Her sister Ethel did become housekeeper for their brother Arthur who took charge of Stanley Mill at Colne. They lived at Ash Mount House, Colne.*

418 Exchange Street, Emporia, Kansas Sat. night *(Late Jan. 1896)*
(Helen Whitworth to her Mother)

My dear Mother,

I will commence my letter tonight then it will be sure to get sent off. I was so surprised to receive yours of the 15th this afternoon. I suppose Ethel will be at Heaton Mersey this weekend. The girls are indeed having a gay time. Emporia people would die if they had so much gaiety. If they are out three evenings they are done up. I don't wonder that the ladies feel tired, as most of them do their own wash. I don't know how they keep their hands so nice, mine have been pretty decent, but this week they commenced to bother me again and I have to use the oiled silk. The linen buttons you sent me are a great curiosity and I show them to most of my visitors. How do you think the blouse looks in the photo, I think it rather nice. I am getting a regular American in the way of wearing wrappers, they are so comfortable that many a time I wear one all day, even now I have a sateen one on, for though it is not far from zero outside we keep the sitting room and kitchen so warm I do not feel the cold. I get up once in the night to replenish the sittingroom fire so though the kitchen gets cold I always have one warm room to go into in the morning. I always lay the kitchen fire at night, then in the morning I light it and go back to bed till the kettle and the porridge boils. It does not take many minutes to lay the table and get breakfast ready, I can assure you.

Uncle John has not said anything yet about my leaving except that it would be difficult to find someone to fill my place. We have got on splendidly together and it is pleasant to feel I have been able to do things even if I am not clever and able to speak three languages. I cannot say yet about coming out again. If only it was not such a distance from you all. I feel so lonely some days though I have so many kind friends around me. The children are very easy to manage, except Jack, and he has arrived at that trying age in a boy, when he thinks he is a man, and a very clever one, and would like to boss over everyone, so we have to take him down a peg. The school term finished yesterday and all the children passed and will be moved into higher classes tomorrow. They teach them quite differently here to at home. I do not like the system so well.

I commenced china painting last week and had two lessons. I did a plate and a bonbon box. It is a rather expensive accomplishment, china is such a price here and the paints are very expensive, but will last a long time. I pay 2/6d. for a lesson of four hours, but can learn a lot in that time especially as I can already do watercolours, the trouble is that the colours change so in firing, that is the chief thing to learn. My teacher is a friend* so the lessons are very pleasant and we are all to ourselves, she teaches in the mornings, but as I could not go then, she gives me whatever afternoon I can get off. I thought I would learn, as it pays well here and may be useful someday to me at home.

I was so glad to hear a little of what is being done at Colne. I also thought of the dances, what a change since then. Aunt Cissie's letter must have amused you. Our relations have funny ways and I expect they think ditto. I don't quite understand what Polly means to do, is she going to live by herself and what will she do with all the furniture, silver etc.? She means to be a long way from her home. It must feel very different to her now and one can't but feel sorry. I should enjoy an afternoon with Aunt Hoyle and hear her ideas. I hope you saw a good company in *Trilby* as I did and enjoyed it as much.

You must be busy dressmaking. I am looking forward to the time when I shall have an evening dress once more, I am waiting for summer now so that I can wear the crepon one you sent me. I do not intend to buy a woollen dress while I am in Kansas as the material is more expensive, the dress-makers are very good and charge accordingly. I owe Aunt Helena 2/6d. so when you next see her will you pay up for me, it is not worth my while getting a postal order for that sum.

Is the new organ paid for yet? If not Mr. Burrowes ought to do like they are doing at the church here. The minister won't let them play on it until it is paid for and each Sunday he says no money no organ, it did amuse me at first.

Did you have the Dead March lately in memory of Prince Henry?** I first heard of his death on Thursday morning, a man in one of the stores told me, as he knew I was English.

I hope you are keeping well and that Flos. is alright, I quite thought she would write me from Colne. I do hope Arthur will be able to find a house, I do not know why he needs such a big one. It would only be trouble to look after. I am finishing this on Sunday afternoon and must close as the P.O. closes at 4p.m. and Walter is waiting to take my letters.

With very much love from your loving child, Helen.

Her teacher was Mrs John D. Graham, née Anne Welles. She was born in Quincy, Illinois 15th. Jan.1870. She came to Emporia, Kansas as a bride in April 1895. She taught oil, watercolour and china painting in an art studio connected to the bookstore at 613 Commercial St. The John D. Graham Art and Book Store sold not only artists materials and books but also wallpaper, mouldings, interior decorations and picture frames. In the Emporia Gazette 19th. December 1920 it noted that ' Perhaps no other woman is more popular with the girls and young women of the town than Mrs. Graham.' Her husband was Clerk of the District Court 1917–23, Chairman of the Food Conservation Movement and a Freemason. They were both members of the First Congregational Church. The art and bookstore closed in 1915 and after that John D. Graham became agent for the New England Life Insurance Co. They lived at 614 Market St. and kept an old fashioned garden full of flowers. They moved out to a farm in the Twin Mound district S.E. of Emporia, (near to the district 75 schoolhouse) on the way to Olpe, in 1937, and then they moved to the Masonic Home in Wichita in 1940. They frequently returned to Emporia – most notably to celebrate their golden wedding 4th April 1945. They had no children. Mrs. Graham was a lifelong friend and correspondent of Helen Whitworth.

** *Prince Henry Maurice of Battenberg 1858–1896, third son of Prince Alexander of Hesse, married to Beatrice, youngest daughter of Queen Victoria. He volunteered with the Ashanti expeditionary force and died of fever.*

418 Exchange Street, Emporia, Kansas March 8th. 1896
(Helen Whitworth to her sister Hilda)

My dearest Hilda
They have all gone to church and it is my turn to cook dinner and I am going to try to do it and write to you at the same time. I feel rather sleepy as it was 1 a.m. before we got to bed, we were so late home from the Normal. The Society Jack is a member of did very well and won the first

prize in the debate and the prize in the Dramatic. You should have heard the noise, 1,200 people can make a pretty big one and each society had a war cry of it's own.

I was looking through my box yesterday and came upon another photo. It is too pale, but as you said you wanted one I will send it today. I hope you received the Emporia papers. Many thanks for the *'Modern Society'* I read it at intervals last week and passed it on to Mrs. Frith yesterday. I have been reading Jan MacLaren's books lately: *'The silence of Dean Mailland'* they are getting more new books in the library soon, I am keeping a look out for them.

Have you finished writing out the receipt book? Mine is getting to want doing, but I think I will leave it for you to do as your writing is so much easier to read than mine.

I am glad you enjoyed the dramatic, did you go to the pantomime, have any of you been to the Opera yet? I think Jack must be very nice, he seems to be so kind to all of you. When I come home I shall have to call him Mr. Marsh at first.

I am sending you this letter home as you did not seem quite sure whether you would be going to Colne or not. How we shall miss Colne Hall, it will look funny to see it empty, I just hate to think about it.

I am going to take the *Strand Magazine* this year, it seems pretty good and it is nice having all those short stories in it.

I am having one painting lesson a week. I enjoy them so much. We shall have to go out to the farm towards the end of May, then I shall have to practice by myself. This is a very short letter in reply to your two long ones, but I have not much news. Have you seen any of the rubber belting yet? I got some in Kansas City and it is quite a success, it is too expensive to be common at present. If it is a new thing at home I will send some when I get a chance.

With much love, dear Hilda, from your loving sister, Helen.

To Keystone Palace Car Co. The Rookery, Chicago, Illinois
(from John Whitworth)
Emporia, Kansas. Apl. 22 1896

Dear Sir,

I intend shipping a car load of horses to Liverpool, England by the *'Georgie'* sailing from New York May 10th. What is the lowest price you could let me have a car for from here to New York?

Yours truly,

John Whitworth.

**THE LETTERS
PART VII**

April–September 1896

THE EMPORIA DAILY GAZETTE *(p.4, col.1) Wednesday 22nd April 1896*

HIS SKULL FRACTURED

JOHN WHITWORTH'S SKULL IS FRACTURED BY A KICK FROM A COLT

John Whitworth a prominent citizen of this town living at the corner of Fifth Avenue and Exchange Street met with a serious accident this morning at 8 o'clock. His skull is fractured and the bones of the right side of his face are fractured by a kick from a colt he was trying to harness, preparatory to driving on his ranch four miles east of town. A physician was sent for and his family notified. A consultation of doctors was held and at 11 o'clock they seemed to think that Whitworth's chances of recovery were few. Mr. Whitworth is a well-known horse buyer, who makes a speciality of fine horses in Kansas. He has shipped many horses to England.

Dr Page, who was assisting Dr. Gardiner in the case of John Whitworth returned at 3.30 this afternoon from the Whitworth ranch and says Mr. Whitworth is still living though very badly injured. Twelve pieces of bone were removed from above the right eye. The skull is fractured and for some time the doctors were hindered in their work by a haemorrhage of the brain, which they finally succeeded in stopping. Still it is impossible to say how soon the haemorrhage will start again. Dr Gardiner is constantly with his patient who has been placed under the influence of morphine.

Mr. Whitworth has five children who have been attending school in Emporia. His wife died about two years ago.

EMPORIA REPUBLICAN *April 24 1896*

IT MAY BE FATAL

JOHN WHITWORTH KICKED IN THE HEAD BY A HORSE

John Whitworth was kicked by a horse and probably fatally injured Wednesday morning at his farm six miles east of town on the Sixth Avenue Road.

He was preparing to ship a lot of horses to the eastern market and at the time of the accident was training a colt. He was driving the animal and running behind it, when it kicked and landed on his forehead crushing the skull. He was carried to the house and two physicians were hastily summoned from town. A part of the skull has been removed. The patient is in a very critical condition and at noon it was thought he could not recover. Mr. Whitworth is about 45 years old, and since the death of his wife about one year ago, he has been living in town at Fourth Avenue and Exchange Street. He has two young children who are going to school. He has been devoting his time of late to buying and selling horses.

The doctors returned from the farm in the afternoon and reported that the injured man was still unconscious. The horse's hoof struck him over the left eye cutting a long deep gash. When the doctors arrived the brains were oozing out. There is very little hope of his recovery.

EMPORIA GAZETTE *(p.1, col.1) Friday April 24th 1896*

John Whitworth's condition is considerably improved today. He may rally and recover yet.

EMPORIA GAZETTE *(p.1, col.1) Tuesday April 28th 1896*

JOHN WHITWORTH WORSE

Dr. Gardiner received call at 12 o'clock last night to attend Mr. Whitworth who was kicked by a horse last week. Mr. Whitworth was sinking this afternoon. After today's visit Dr. Gardiner is reported to have said that he could see no change for the better. Mr. Whitworth's condition had very much improved the last few days. The sudden change bodes no good.

(Helen Whitworth told her daughter, years later, that he might have recovered if she had not had to move him to the storm shelter when a tornado threatened – the storm shelter was dug into the hillside below the house.)

EMPORIA DAILY GAZETTE *(p.4, col.2) Friday May 1st 1896*

JOHN WHITWORTH DEAD

AFTER SEVERAL DAYS OF SUFFERING HE PASSES AWAY

John Whitworth, who was kicked in the head and face by a horse last week died last night.

The deceased was born in England 50 years ago. He was the son of Benjamin Whitworth, philanthropist and a Member of Parliament.

155

Mr Whitworth came to this country and settled in Lyon County twelve years ago with a wife and four children John, aged 16, Mary, aged 18, Daisy, aged 14, and Walter, aged 12. Since then Gladys, the youngest child was born. Mrs. Whitworth died two years ago.

The orphan children have the sympathy of the entire community. The funeral services will be held at 9.30 o'clock tomorrow at the Congregational Church, and will be conducted by the Rev. Busser.

EMPORIA DAILY REPUBLICAN May 1st. 1896

JOHN WHITWORTH DEAD

Passed away at 5 o'clock last evening from the effects of his injury. John Whitworth, who was kicked in the head by a horse one week ago last Wednesday, died from his injury at his farm five miles east of the town on Sixth Avenue Road at 5 o'clock last night. At first there was little or no hope of his recovery, but notwithstanding the serious nature of the wound the surgical operation was successful and for several days the chances of his recovery had been considered good. Lately however mortification set in and death soon resulted.

Mr. Whitworth's wife died very suddenly about one year ago, and now the five children are left orphans. Since the death of their mother the children have resided with their father's niece, Miss Helen Whitworth, at the corner of Forth Avenue and Exchange Street.

The late John Whitworth, whose death yesterday is so generally lamented, was born in England fifty years ago. He was the son of the well-known philanthropist, Benjamin Whitworth, who for many years was a prominent member of the British House of Commons. Mr. Whitworth came to Lyon County about 12 years ago and purchased the Whitley Farm where he was residing at the time of his death. He leaves five children, the oldest 18 years and the youngest 11 years to mourn his sudden untimely departure. Everyone who had dealings with the late John Whitworth found him a man of the strictest honour and integrity and in losing him Lyon County has sustained the loss of a valuable and most highly respected citizen.

The funeral will take place from the First Congregational Church tomorrow morning at 11 o'clock. The Rev. S.E.Busser will conduct the services. Private services will be held at the house at 9.30.

EMPORIA DAILY GAZETTE Saturday May 2nd. 1896 (p.1, col.4)

THE FUNERAL OF JOHN WHITWORTH

The funeral service of John Whitworth was held by Rev. S.E.Busser at the First Congregational Church this morning at 11 o'clock. A short private

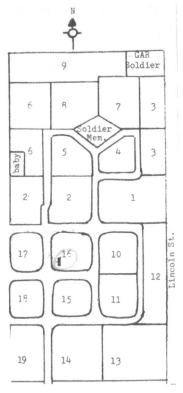

Plan of the Maplewood Cemetery showing location of graves

service was held at 10.30 at the residence east of the city. Rev. Busser chose for his text Revelation 22, 5. 'And there shall be no night there'. His sermon breathed hope and consolation to the bereaved family. Rev. Busser spoke of Mr. Whitworth, their father, and explained that though his life was bright and full of happiness in this world yet he had gone to a world where there is no darkness, but where all is light.

The pall bearers were L.T. Heritage, Harvey Frith, Howard Dunlap, J.N. Wilkinson, J.D. Graham, and Mr. Falkner. The interment was made in the Maplewood Cemetery beside the remains of his wife.

The music was furnished by the Congregational Choir composed of Miss Ascah Harris, Mrs Charles Harris, Messrs Edwin Maloy and Geo. Smith.

The floral tributes were numerous and beautiful. The grave was lined and covered with flowers.

He was buried beside his wife in the Maplewood Cemetery, Block 16, Lot N1/2 45, on 2nd May 1896. The inscription on the memorial stone reads:

John Whitworth died 30 April 1896 aged 50 years;
'Blessed are the dead that rest in the Lord for they shall
rest from their labours, and their works do follow them.'

A Manchester paper (not specified) in the Manchester Library Newspaper cuttings collection gave the following obituary notice:

John Whitworth
Mr John Whitworth, second son of the late Mr. Benjamin Whitworth died at Emporia, Kansas having bought a large farm at Emporia, and it was

from a kick of a horse there that he died on April 30th. Whilst in Manchester he took little part in public affairs but was actively associated for some time with Mr. -William O'Hanlon in the management of the Heyrod St. mission in Ancoats. Mr. Whitworth in 1877

Whitworth graves in the Maplewood Cemetery, Emporia

married Miss Haworth, sister of Mr. Abraham Haworth, who died two years ago and he leaves a family of two sons and three daughters. Mr. Thomas Whitworth goes out on the -Britannic *next Wednesday for the purpose of bringing them home to this country.*

Telegram Western Union Telegraph Company
Received 526 Commercial St., Emporia, Kansas. 7 May 1896

Whitworth, Manchester
Received letter leaving Britannic Wednesday write care Herron
Father

Telegram Western Union Telegraph Company
Received 526 Commercial St., Emporia, Kansas. 7 May 1896

Very grieved much sympathy write us fully Haworth

1, Greenbank, Waterloo. May 2nd. 1896
(Elizabeth Whitworth to her daughter Helen)

My dear Helen,
We were all paralysed at the news we had yesterday. Aunt Bessie wrote to Papa as soon as they had Jack's telegram. Now it looks so long before we can have any letters from you with particulars. Arthur writes me that he knows you are quite capable of looking after things and he says

someone must go out to help you all. I feel I would like to do so much to help you and I am quite powerless.

Papa has gone to Manchester to see Uncle James (*Boyd*) and the Haworths, so when he gets back we shall know what has been arranged. The children will feel their loss, it is sad for them without both father and mother. It seems so short a time since the latter died (nearly two years). I suppose you will have to go back to the farm to look after things there. You must not do too much and so impair your health. I expect Falkner will help you as he will know so much about things. Anyhow you must have some help. You cannot work both your brain and your hands too much.

We are all very well but the weather is cold, not at all like May Day. The relations seem to get fewer very fast. Aunt Ellen is in a very delicate state, she has been in hospital again. She was in the Isle of Man (Port Erin) at Easter and was taken ill there she scarcely expected to get back home again.

All unite in best love to you and the children. I cannot say more everything is so full of sorrow.

Your loving Mother.

P.O. Emporia, Kansas. May 9th 1896
(Helen Whitworth to her sister Hilda)

My darling Hilda,

I am going to write to you this time, whether it is your turn or not, I have been writing to Mother lately because of sending the letters on to other relatives. It is rather strange that Arthur and I should both be left to look after an uncle's business, and within so short a time. We are only just beginning to realise that Uncle John has gone from us. It is a good thing we cannot see ahead, or I should never have dared to come out to Kansas. I shall always be glad that I did as Uncle John got so much more contented when he found that I could manage things. What a mercy we all learned to keep accounts when we were little. The judge was telling me how to do it and seemed quite surprised when I told him that I had kept them for years. Last Sunday there was no service at the Congregational Church, and we did not want to go to any other. We drove out to the cemetery to see if all had been left nice, and it did look so pretty and peaceful. Some of our friends had arranged the flowers so beautifully over both graves. We left Gladys at home as she was not feeling well, her illness developed into measles, and she has been in bed until today. Fortunately it was only a mild attack and she is coming downstairs again tomorrow. April was the hottest April for 29 years and May is going to be ditto at the rate it is going at present. I can't put on much thinner clothes, so I suppose I must be content to melt.

Fortunately the nights are fairly cool. I have had a man here two days fixing all the screens over the doors and windows, even with them the flies are getting pretty thick, and the mosquitoes and wasps have come so early this year, they are a torment. Please thank Ethel for the papers and letters ... I hope you are keeping well. I put your letter away somewhere and can't find it so if I forget to answer any questions forgive me this once.

J Harvey Frith's Office, Sat. morn.

I had not time to finish your letter at home so will do it here. I could not help smiling this morning on the way to town as I thought of the different conveyances I had come in since Saturday. Last Saturday was the Closed Carriage; Sunday, the Surrey; Monday, the Hay Rack; Tuesday, the Spring Wagon, Wednesday, the Road Cart; and today the heavy Farm Wagon. I will write again very soon, thanks for the papers and *Modern Society*. With very much love from your loving sister, Helen Whitworth.

Tuesday June 2nd 1896
(Helen Whitworth to her sister Hilda)

My dearest Hilda,

I see Father has written to Mother so I will write to you. I owe you so many letters I am afraid they will never be repaid. We have been having horrid weather the last few days, so dull, Father likes it better as, being cool, he feels more comfortable. He has his breakfast in bed every day. I am beginning to get used to doing up his bedroom sometime after the other work is finished. He thinks this is a terrible place, so uncivilised. He was growling at a man yesterday about the roads, saying what good roads we have in England. The man listened quietly and then said 'Mr. Whitworth, your roads have been getting made for some hundreds of years, and ours are not 30 years old yet, and our little state is a good bit larger to look after than all your country, but if you will come back in 100 years I guess our roads will be better than yours.' Father seems to spend a good bit of his time picking up kindling, he says everything is so untidy, and how he expects it to be anything else with Uncle John and one man to oversee 200 acres I don't know. He confessed yesterday that 'Bevadlia' used to look pretty bad sometimes with two men and himself doing it. I believe the climate and the quiet life will do Father a lot of good, he is looking quite sunburnt already, and better in himself now his leg is better. He goes to bed between 9 and 10 every night. I am sure being away from the Clubs for a while will do him good. Can you believe it? He hasn't had his stamps out yet, wonders will never cease. I hope we shall soon decide when we shall be able to leave, for though Father can see after a good deal of the business, I have to bother with it as well, and there is so much to do and think about every day, I feel as though it would be such a relief to mind and body if I had nothing to do or think about for a few weeks, and did not know beforehand what I was going to have to eat.

The packing up will be a terrible job. We will soon have to begin and look through some of the clothes etc. I wish I knew what the children were going to do in England, as then I could decide about household linen etc. We shall have to have a sale, and it will take two days, and at sales here they provide dinners for all comers. I feel sorry to leave Mrs. Frith, we are great friends, and I am her only friend in Emporia. She had been to the graves before us last Saturday and made the graves look so pretty. May and I took a large boxful of flowers and put them all about. It was just a month from the funeral, it felt more like a year. This house does not feel like home now, and it has been a very pleasant home for me as Uncle John did all he could to make me happy and feel that it was another home. Yet I feel more thankful every day that Uncle J. did not live, as he would never have been able to live the active life he liked, and we would always have been in fear of softening of the brain coming on.

Please thank Ethel for her long letter, you all seem to have gone bicycle mad. Ethel Hollinger's letter was half full of learning to ride the bike. May and I have wanted to learn but they charge so much for hiring.

I haven't found the veils yet, you must have packed them away in a safe place.

Please tell Mother that the skirt fits to perfection and the blouse is also very comfortable, it is a little wide across the chest but I don't think I shall alter it. I cut out the alpaca blouse today, and I got quite a good bit sewn this afternoon, I am copying a pattern out of '*The Princess*' and will send it to you when I have finished, then you will have an idea what the dress looks like. I wore the gloves last Sunday. I shall be writing again soon, so will close for this time with very much love to you & all the others.

I am dear Hilda, your loving sister, Helen Whitworth.

P.O. Emporia, Kansas July 8th. 1896
(Helen Whitworth to her sister Hilda)

My dear Hilda,

Father has written to Mother, as I have only a few minutes before he goes to town I will scrawl a few lines to you. Tell Mother I will write a long letter for the next mail. I ought to have gone this morning to spend the day with Mrs. Graham but it came on a heavy shower after breakfast so I shall have to defer my visit to next week. I am sorry to hear that Florence has been ill, and hope she is better again. How did she manage to get such a chill? We are fairly well, the heat last week was fairly trying when we were busy, but this week is comparatively cool. The children went to town yesterday to have their photos taken. I treated them to ice-creams. I made Gladys such a pretty white dress last week, altogether with the ribbon and embroidery it only cost 7/10d. Father is going round trying to kill flies with a newspaper. He does not inflict that on us much as the flies are too many for him. That shipwreck was indeed a terrible thing, we first heard of it two Sundays ago, but hoped it was not as bad as the papers said then.

We shall have to think of looking through the various rooms and putting together the belongings we want to take. I hate seeing the place and everything sold, but if it has to be then I don't care how soon it is all over. I don't know what the Haworths are thinking or mean to do, I don't approve of their boarding school plan for the girls, at any rate they might let them go to a day school for a time. The poor children will feel homesick at having to see all go here and as it were start a new life altogether. I think it would be cruel to send them off to different places especially as they are so fond of home. They get homesick if they are away for three days staying with friends.

Well, I must close, with heaps of love dear, from Helen.

P.O. Emporia, Kansas, Sunday night *(August 1896)*
(Helen Whitworth to her sister Hilda)

My dearest Hilda,

I was so pleased to get such a long letter from you yesterday, and am glad you and Mother had such a nice time at Porton. We have really decided now for the date of the sale, and then we shall leave as soon as possible afterwards. I don't know yet which way we shall go home, and don't care much. We have commenced packing up. Did two cases the other day, the thermometer standing at 100 in the room where I was. It has been very hot for some time, but since Thursday it has been a regular sirocco. We have had to keep all the south windows closed during the day, the wind scorched things so. All the late corn is ruined, it has all burnt up. Fortunately ours was ready for cutting so it does not matter so much for us. The trouble is that it does not look a bit like rain, and until it does we may expect the hot winds and the thermometer round 100.

The Whitworth children in the summer of 1896, before returning home

I must be getting a regular salamander for today I cooked dinner, walked two miles over the prairie to Sunday School, and two miles back, and then got tea ready. Of course I had not many clothes on and what I had got a little damp, but I don't find the heat worse when I am moving around than when I am sitting still. Lying down is uncomfortable, as the perspiration rolls off one. I could not help laughing when I went to waken the others yesterday, for Father was the only one with his head in the usual place. We all had pushed our heads into the middle of the rooms where we could get a draught, and everybody had their heads where their feet should be, and not even a sheet over them. Gladys and I have used a sheet only twice this month.

I did not expect to write to you till Wednesday but as we can send letters in with some visitors who have come out I thought I would enclose this in Father's. I will write to Mother next Saturday.

Oh, my, wont it be nice to see you again, and what lots we shall have to talk about. One thing I shan't like is so many houses around me. Our nearest neighbours are ½ mile away and we can't see their house, and it will seem funny having so many neighbours.

We had a very pleasant day on Thursday when Miss Gillet came and spent the day with us, it was so hot, we decided to go down to the timber and have our supper there. Queenie took some photographs of the house and grounds for us, then we all went wading in the river and she took a snapshot of us in the river, we must look pretty. She has promised us all one, so you will be able to see it someday soon.

Father and I were in town yesterday afternoon. We brought home two watermelons so have been feasting today. We also had our first grapes for supper. Father rather spoilt the vines as he cut too much of the foliage off, and here they want to be as much covered with leaves as possible as the sun is too hot and shrivels up the berries.

I am glad Ethel was successful in the tennis, I shall have to learn it all over again, it will be quite funny. I expect the Shaws would enjoy their visit, have they got any young men yet? I wonder if Arthur will be in his new house when we get back. I do think the Haworth's are behaving very funnily, they will find that the children mean to have a say in the matter. Mrs Haworth has not much idea of managing children. We have not had any letters from them for six weeks so don't know any plans. No time for more, this mail.

Give my love to all, and with heaps of love to yourself from your loving sister, Helen.

The following Emporia newspaper cuttings were kept with the letters, and date to the summer of 1896.

A Runaway

Last evening a team belonging to the Misses Whitworth collided with the team attached to the delivery wagon belonging to J.G. Williams and caused the latter to 'tear up the dirt'. It only ran a short distance but was successful in partially demolishing the wagon. The ladies sent a blacksmith to the store and left orders for him to adjust the loss to the owner of the wagon.

Farm to let

Four miles east of Emporia, residence of the late John Whitworth, excellent stonehouse and outbuildings. 150 acres bottom land and 200 acres of pasture well watered. Cash rental $600. Sale of stock and household effects Sept. 9th. Apply on the premises.

P.O. Emporia, Kansas, U.S.A. Friday night *(late August 1896)*
(Helen Whitworth to her sister Hilda)

My dear Hilda,

I will commence my letter tonight as tomorrow (all being well) Father and I leave for Kansas City by the 11.30 train, arriving there at 4.30. I shall have to come back on Monday morning, Father will stay till Tuesday. It seems scarcely worth the trouble but I want to see Miss McDonald again and I also have to get Daisy a jacket, they have not got the winter stock in here yet and Daisy can't do without till she gets to England as she has not any, hers being too small and only about right for Gladys.

Just fancy a month from today I will be talking 16 to the dozen. It seems too good to be true that I shall see you all again. All our packing cases leave on Wednesday, so we shall be busy on Tuesday fastening them up, then will come the boxes to be done. I just feel so tired and the busy time has not come yet, and I am so afraid of forgetting something. When I get home I shall have to set to and make a new rig out for Sundays as my winter dresses are getting rather old style. I have not altered one of them since I left home. I did try to get a new sleeve pattern a short time ago, but could not find one to suit. I thought once of having a winter dress made here but decided it would only get crushed.

Yesterday was quite a busy day. In the morning I got the china that we are taking home packed, then Jack and I took it to town after dinner, to leave it to be repacked. While we were away five callers arrived, we found them still there and they stayed to supper. The children were invited out to a birthday party about 3 miles from here. Jack would not go, and May said she would not drive in the dark so I had to leave washing up the supper dishes and go with them to drive. We did not get home till after 11p.m. then we had the horses to unhitch and put in the stable, so it was midnight before we got to bed.

The children are beginning to realise that they are really leaving their home, I know how much they will miss it, and feel so sorry for them. Last Sunday we had Mr. and Mrs. Falconer and Mr. Orlter round for the day and Mr. and Mrs. Graham came, and all stayed till nearly 10p.m. as it was such a lovely moonlight night. Since Saturday we have been having such delightful cool weather, the sun and moon both seem to shine through the cloud, it makes me think there must be some big forest fires as it was like this once before when there was.

I am so sorry to hear you had such a bad throat & hope you are feeling better again. Has Mother gone to Colne yet? It was very sad about Mrs. Smith. Florrie Smith is Ethel's great friend isn't she? I do not know any of them. What a sell about the *Lucania*, it would have made me cross if I had gone that far for nothing, especially when I had taken people along. It is funny that we happen to sail on the *Britannic*, and the cabin is next but one to the one I came in. I wonder if there will be many passengers on, and also if there will be equinoxial gales. I shall feel as if I have nothing to do at first, when I haven't any cooking to do. We churn and bake every other day. I generally see after the bread, but though I get the churn ready, I only do the churning on Tuesdays. We are making heaps of butter now, it is nice having plenty for cooking ...

16th August 1896
(Helen Whitworth to her sister Hilda)

My dearest Hilda,

I hope you got the scrawl I sent you last week, I wrote in such a hurry. I was afraid you would not be able to read half. We were quite surprised to get another letter from home on Tuesday, also the papers etc. ... I read the novelette that afternoon. It is a year yesterday since Grandma Shaw's funeral, and two years yesterday since I left home and I have been packing my box again to come home. Gladys has been watching me. It is not quite as easy to pack up for seven people as it was for myself. We want to get as much as possible done this month, then we can go out the last few days and just before the sale we shall be awfully busy. We have to give a free lunch to all that come. As soon as everything is sold we shall have to go to town to board there for a few days.

I wonder if I shall be home in time for a picnic to Hightown before it gets too cold, it is the nicest month here.

Tell Alice to write and tell me about her visit to Ramsay. I have no news, so with much love from your loving sister, Helen.

The winding up of John Whitworth's estate

Various papers have survived which give an indication of how the process of winding up John Whitworth's affairs progressed through the summer of 1896, and they give an insight into the stock and equipment on the farm. Helen Whitworth applied for and was granted letters of administration for John Whitworth's estate on 5th May 1896, by the Probate Judge, F.M.Chapee. Her attorney was the family friend, J. Harvey Frith. John Whitworth died intestate leaving 'two farms in Lyon County, Kansas, one of 320 acres, more or less, and one of 350 acres, more or less; and personal property consisting of cattle, livestock, wagons, buggies, farm machinery and household furniture' at an estimated value of $8,100. At the same time Helen Whitworth was also appointed administratrix for the estate of Marian Whitworth.

A paper dated 12th May 1896 details the allowance to the children exempt from the administration and debts of the deceased John

Whitworth: 2 cows, 10 hogs, 1 team of horses, 20 sheep, 200 bushels of corn in the crib, school books and family library, lot in burial ground, wearing apparel and family beds and bedding, cooking stove and appendages, and implements of husbandry all necessary for the use of the children, and the family piano.

The following articles were allowed with appraisement:

Household goods and furniture	estimate of value	$350.00
5 wagons	.. ..	50.00
3 cultivators	.. ..	30.00
2 harrows	.. ..	2.00
Harness and tackle for teams	.. ..	37.00
1 Sacey ($25), 2 cars ($10), 1 sprung wagon ($18)	.. ..	53.00
1 Go Devil and Stacker ($10), 1 Corn cutter ($12),		
1 Lister ($12), 2 Mowers ($ 30)	.. ..	64.00
1 Platform scale, 1 Planet Drill,		
2 sets of block and tackle	.. ..	5.00
Various articles more or less out of repair	.. ..	50.00
Aggregate value		$291.00

In addition John Whitworth held notes of the following Mortgages granted to

F.H. Fish and Etta Fish	23 June 1895	$93.56
W.H. Falconer	Feb. 1895	$40.00
Mrs. F. Burfort & V.J.Packman	18 Dec 1895	$35.00
W.J. Walters	23 Nov. 1895	$50.00
E. Alexander and A. Alexander	25 June 1895	$50.00

In cash he had $2,163.31.

The formal description of his land holdings was as follows:

Acres	Section	Township	Range	County	State
80	4	19	12	Lyon	Kansas
160	4	19	12		
80	4	19	12		
351	8	19	1		

Total acreage: 671

ADMINISTRATRIX SALE

To be sold at public auction **without** reserve, at the farm of the late John Whitworth, 4 miles east of Emporia, on

September 9th and 10th. '96

Commencing at 10 o'clock a. m., the following stock and property:

3 1-year-old Steers, 10 2-year-old Steers
25 3-year-old Steers
1 2-year-old Pedigree Jersey Bull
4 Pedigree Jersey Cows, 3 Pedigree Jersey Heifers
6 Good Milch Cows, 2 Half-bred Jersey Heifers
1 Pedigree Jersey Bull Calf
5 Pedigree Jersey Heifer Calves
4 Half-bred Jersey Heifer Calves
3 Half-bred Jersey Bull Calves
1 English Shire 7-year-old Mare "Leake Mettle" and Colt
1 Clydesdale 4-year-old Mare "Lassie"
4 Work Mares, 2 4-year-old Horses, (broken)
1 Gray Mare (aged) and Colt, 5 4-year-old Colts
4 3-year-old Colts, 3 2-year-old Colts
7 yearling Colts, 1 Donkey and Cart

1 Poland China Boar, 1 Poland China Brood Sow
2 Poland China young Sows
2 Poland China young Boars
30 Breeding Sows and Hogs and Poultry
2 Hay, and 2 Lumber Wagons, 1 Spring Wagon
1 Surrey, 2 Road Carts
2 Mowing Machines, 2 Hay Rakes
1 Corn Planter, 2 Cultivators, 1 Lister
1 Disc Cultivator, 3 Plows, 1 Harrow
1 Sweep Rake, 1 Hay Stacker
Quantity of Timber and Shingles
About 1,600 bushels old Corn in Crib
40 Acres of Corn, 8 Acres Sorgum, 15 Tons Millett
Quantity Kaffir Corn, 3 Acres Potatoes
About 60 Tons Alfalfa
Household Effects and Furniture
1 Piano (new) 7 Octave, by Harvard, Boston

And other articles too numerous to mention
Stock will be sold **September 9th.** Furniture, etc. will be sold September 10th.

TERMS OF SALE.

Sums under $10 net cash, sums over $10 six months credit on approved bankable paper, subject if then unpaid, to 10 per cent interest from date of sale. Steers and hogs to be sold for net cash. Other purchases subject to 5 per cent discount for cash.

FREE LUNCH.

Tom Scofield, AUCTIONEER.

HELEN WHITWORTH,
ADMINISTRATRIX.

The poster advertising the sale of the farm, 9th and 10th September 1896

Helen Whitworth was granted permission by Judge Chappee to sell the personal belongings and property of John Whitworth in a private sale, rather than a public one.

The poster for the sale at the farm on the 9th and 10th September lists the following stock and property:-

3 1 year old steers

10 2 year old steers

25 3 year old steers

1 2 year old pedigree Jersey Bull

4 pedigree Jersey Cows,
3 pedigree Jersey Heifers
1 pedigree Jersey Bull calf
3 pedigree Jersey Heifer calves
2 Halfbred Jersey Heifer calves
3 Halfbred Jersey Bull calves
1 English Shire 7 year old Mare 'Leake Mettle' and colt
1 Clydesdale 4 year old Mare 'Lassie'
4 Work Mares
2 4 year old horses (broken)
1 Gray Mare (aged) and colt
5 4 year old Colts
4 3 year old Colts
8 2 year old Colts
7 yearling Colts
1 Donkey and cart
1 Poland China Boar
1 Poland Breeding Sow
2 Poland Young Sows
2 Poland Young Boars
30 Breeding Sows and Hogs
Poultry
2 Hay and 2 Lumber wagons, and 1 Spring wagon
1 Surrey, 2 Road Carts
2 Mowing Machines, 2 Hay Rakes,
1 Corn Planter, 2 Cultivators, 1 Lister
1 Disc Cultivator, 3 Plows, 1 Harrow
1 Sweep Rake, 1 Hay Stacker,
Quantity of Timber and Shingles
About 1,500 bushels of old Corn in the Crib
45 acres of Corn, 8 acres Sorghum, 15 tons Millet
Quantity of Kaffir Corn, 2 Acres Potatoes,
About 60 tons Alfalfa
Household effects and Furniture
1 Piano (new) 7 octave by Harvard, Boston.

Helen Whitworth paid Thomas Schofield $40 for crying the sale at the farm on 9th and 10th September 1896. It is not known how many people she had to provide with free lunches. The house and land were sold to Henry Korte who came from Jefferson, Kentucky, with his family. On 12th September 1896 Mary Whitworth signed the sale of the farm and most of the land in Section 8 to Henry Korte; her one fifth share amounting to $1,800 (the other children were too young to sign for themselves). The land in the S.E. Quarter of the S.E. Quarter of Section 8 (with the exception of 1/2 acre belonging to P.C. Cowling) was sold to Charles S. Cross and Kate Hilda Cross on 10th September 1896 for a total of $1,150. The land in the south half of Section 4 was sold to Frank G. Wecker and Bertha Wecker in March 1900 for $2,560 plus $640 which was paid separately to Mary Whitworth. As for the household possessions, W.A. White, editor of the Emporia Gazette, wrote to Gladys Mackennal, *née* Whitworth, in 1942 'an old chest that carried the name Mary Bore or Bohr was sold at auction and a neighbour bought it (Marshall Warren, the chest was dated 1630). We bought the brass andirons with lovely knobs. We gave them to our son, Bill, who still has them'.

On 12th September 1896 L.T. Heritage petitioned Judge Chappee for letters of Administration for John Whitworth's estate at the request of the present Administratorix, Helen Whitworth, as she was then returning to England with the children. At this time the estate was described as consisting of 'farming implements, carriages, carts, horses, cattle, sheep, marl and corn, promissory notes due the said John Whitworth, and cash estimated to be worth about $5,966. L.T. Heritage was sworn in as Administrator by Judge Chappee on 18th. September 1896. Notice of the Final Settlement of the estate of John Whitworth appeared in the Emporia Republican in April 1898.

Once the sale had been completed little time was lost in setting off for England. They sailed from New York on R.M.S. *Britannic* on 16th September, at 12 noon (Lieut. H.J. Haddock, R.N.R., captain), and reached Liverpool on the 24th. The passage was fairly smooth with a westerly gale causing rough seas only on one day, the 21st.

When the Whitworth children returned home their uncle Jesse Haworth and their cousins Alfred and John Goodier Haworth became their legal guardians.

Woodside, Bowdon, Cheshire. Dec. 14th 1896
(Jesse Haworth to Captain L.T. Heritage)

Dear Sir,

I duly received your draft upon Parr's Bank, London for £83 6/8d for which please accept my thanks.

The Whitworth children are keeping well and seem to be fairly happy and contented. A furnished house was rented for them on their arrival, but

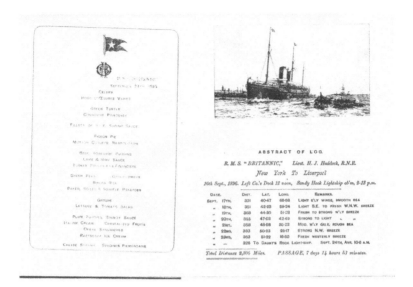

RMS Britannic: *menu and Abstract of Log*

we are now in treaty for a house which they may call their own, as Bowdon appears to suit their health and they are naturally willing to settle amongst their relatives and friends. It is not far from where they resided before going out to America, and one important attraction to them is that it has a little spare land upon which they can keep poultry, and thus have something to remind them of their Kansas farm life.

With all Xmas good wishes, I remain yours faithfully, Jesse Haworth.

Eventually the children moved into Church Bank, Bowdon where they kept house together, with Mary (May) in charge. What happened to each of them, and to the other members of the family who had spent time with them in Kansas, is told in outline in the following Postscript chapter.

Church Bank, Bowdon

The Whitworth children, c. 1898/9

POSTSCRIPT

John Haworth Whitworth D.S.O., M.C. 1879–1918

Jack Whitworth, as he was always known in the family, was born on September 26th 1879 at Alderley Edge, Cheshire. He went to school first in Bowdon at an establishment run by Miss Morris and Miss Croft and here he first met William MacKennal who was to become a lifelong friend and eventually (in 1913) his brother-in-law, and later (in 1918) his biographer. As a child he was high spirited and happy, though with a strong temper which he soon learned to control. At the age of seven he went out to live in Emporia, Kansas with his family. His time in Kansas has been fully covered by the letters, in the preceding

VOTE FOR

WHITWORTH

—— SUPPORT ——

J. H. WHITWORTH
The LIBERAL, LOCAL, and
FREE TRADE CANDIDATE

Vote for Whitworth

chapters. Life on the ranch never really interested him and he was quite glad to return to England.

On his return to England with his brother and sisters they set up home at Church Bank in Bowdon, Cheshire. Immediately on his return in September 1896 he went to Bowdon College to complete his education. He was an able scholar and won an Exhibition to Wadham College, Oxford in 1898, where he read Modern History and then Jurisprudence. He graduated B.A. in 1901, and M.A. in 1911. Whilst at Oxford he took part in debating and literary societies, speaking several times at the Oxford Union. He had acquired a love of oratory at the State Normal College in Emporia, and that combined with a certain strenuousness, rather than a natural aptitude, made him a clear and convincing speaker. He also distinguished himself as a sportsman: he took up rowing and rugby and represented the college in both. He was described by one of his contemporaries in college as 'one of the most popular men in college. In the warmth of this universal appreciation he expanded and developed in a wonderful way... He began to lose his awkwardness and uncouthness.

174

Major John Whitworth

And this process... went on at a continually accelerated pace in after years ... He throve in every respect on success and appreciation.' Another Oxford friend remarked on his stillness and remoteness. His interest in politics, already stirring in Kansas, continued at Bowdon College and at Wadham.

After Oxford he went to London to read for the Bar: he obtained First Class marks in the Bar Examinations in Evidence and Commercial Law. He lived in the Mansfield House Settlement, in Canning Town. Here he was able to get first-hand experience of the social problems of living in a big city.

He helped at the Settlement by giving educational classes, and he started and ran a boxing club. He also managed an organisation called 'The Poor Man's Lawyer'. In the Bar Final Examinations in 1903 he was one of the three who obtained a First Class. Early in the following year he was called to the Bar at the Inner Temple, with a Certificate of Honour, and he started to practice in Manchester.

Here he made a slow start, but when he joined Mr. A.G. Roby's chambers in 1910 he really began to go ahead. He continued to work for the 'Poor Man's Lawyer' and for a similar institution in the Heyrod Street Club in Ancoats. Mr. Roby described him as a 'born advocate' at his best in court when he was fighting with his back to the wall, 'my only fear as to his future success sprang from his keenness for political life.'

As soon as he settled in Manchester he joined the '95 Club and early in 1905 he was elected to its committee: from 1907 to 1909 he served as its secretary and 1912 to 1913 as its chairman. He frequently spoke for the Club at Liberal Club gatherings in and around Manchester. In the General Election of January 1910 he contested Shrewsbury for the Liberal Party. It was a safe Conservative seat but he 'worked indefatigably at visiting, calling from house to house canvassing, and winning much respect for his strong character and sincerity' . He and his sisters made their headquarters in the Crown Hotel for the duration of the campaign. Undaunted by the defeat, he stood again in December 1910 as Liberal

Candidate for Knutsford, Cheshire. This seat had been won for the Liberals in the 1906 election by Mr. Alfred J. King, but had reverted to the Conservatives at the general Election of January 1910. When Mr. Asquith appealed to the country in December 1910, Mr. King decided not to stand, and Jack Whitworth was selected to stand in his place. He fought this election campaign with great energy and enthusiasm but was unable to defeat the sitting Tory member. In the course of this campaign, however, he met his future wife, Ida Mary King, the daughter of Alfred and Julia King of Bollington, and Elleray, Windermere. Their courtship was not without it's difficulties: John was strongly critical of Campbell-Bannerman's premiership, Alfred King had a huge respect for the first Prime Minister under whom he'd served, and even had Campbell-Bannerman's letters to him specially bound in a volume. Also, it was still in the period of arranged marriages and Alfred King had expected his daughter to marry the son of one of his friends. Despite the difficulties, the wedding took place on 12th March 1913 at the Friends Meeting House, Colthouse, near Hawkshead, Cumbria, and it was followed by a large family reception at Elleray, Windermere. They spent their honeymoon at Housell Bay near the Lizard in Cornwall.

They settled in Bowdon, Cheshire, at a house given to them as a wedding present by Jack's uncle, Jesse Haworth, and called Ingersley after Ida King's birthplace. Their first child, Julia Marian, was born on 17th May 1914 and was baptized at Bowdon Downs Congregational Chapel on 21st June 1914 exactly 37 years after her grandparents' wedding there.

Apart from his increasingly successful career as a barrister, he was involved in local affairs. He became Chairman of Bowdon District Council. He worked at the P.S.A., and on the Smallholdings Committee, and for the Vale Penny Bank. He was also a well-known Rugby Union forward, playing for Sale and for the Cheshire County Teams.

The storm clouds of war were already gathering. Jack foresaw the immensity of the coming struggle and the seriousness of the issues involved. After the British retreat from Mons it was clear that every available man would be needed in the army. On September 10th 1914 he joined the Manchester University O.T.C. and after a short period of training he entered the 2/6th (Territorial) Battalion of the Manchester Regiment. He received his Captaincy on 31st. October that year.

For the first two and a half years of the war his work was concerned with training recruits; in 1915 in Southport, in 1916 at Crowborough, Sussex and later at Reed Hall, Colchester. During this time two more daughters were born into his family: Elizabeth Mary in 1915, and Ida Margaret (my mother) in 1916. His youngest daughter, Joan Haworth, was born in 1918.

In 1917 he went to France. Part of the time he was on the Front line with the rest of his Battalion. In July he was awarded the Military Cross for extricating his battalion from an intensive gas shell bombardment whilst crossing the River Ysen (during which he was gassed) and finding another safer crossing at Nieuport Ville. In the autumn of 1917, having attained the rank of Major, he was put in charge of a Brigade reinforcement school for giving final training to soldiers who had never been abroad before, at which he was particularly successful. In October 1917 he became second in command to Col. M. Melville who wrote: 'No C.O. can have a more reliable and loyal second in command, or a more delightful companion to live with. Always cheery, always an optimist and always able to see the amusing side of things however great the discomforts... His unfailing sense of humour, his outspoken and always helpful criticisms and his exceptional gallantry and courage in serious moments will never be forgotten by those who served under him in France.' He was home for Christmas and New Year with his family and then returned to France for what was to prove the last time.

In March 1918 the long-anticipated offensive began, and Jack found himself in command of the Battalion, since the C.O. was on temporary sick leave. As one soldier remarked afterwards 'our Battalion got more than its share of nasty things'. Only seventeen men survived the five day offensive. John held his position, near St. Quentin, under intense shelling and in face of heavy enemy attack until forced to withdraw at the end of two days, for this he was awarded the D.S.O. Three days later, with his command reduced to 34 men, they were again subjected to intense attack and were forced to retreat. Jack was hit in the back by a machine gun bullet and fell. He was taken to the ambulance train by his men and eventually to the 8th General Military Hospital in Rouen. He appeared to be making a good recovery and wrote cheerfully home to friends and family, but suddenly whilst having breakfast on Easter Sunday morning, 31st. March 1918, he collapsed and within 20 minutes had died from his wounds. He was buried in the military cemetery at St. Sever, Rouen.

The news of his death soon reached Emporia, where this notice appeared in the *Emporia Gazette* on 16th May, 1918:

Residents of Lyon County who were acquainted with the Whitworth family who formerly lived east of Emporia, will be sorry to hear of the death from wounds received in battle of the oldest son, Major Jack Whitworth. For gallantly extricating his battalion from a difficult and serious situation, he won the Military Cross... and was in charge of the battalion at the time he received his death wound. By the men of his regiment he was held in high regard, and in the fierce fights in which they shared they asked for no better leader.

The Emporia Gazette *published the following tribute to him:*

He Lived in Emporia

Something more than twenty years ago the Whitworth family moved from Emporia to England. The boy Jack Whitworth was at that time about 16 years old, and went to the Emporia Schools: May Whitworth was graduated in the class of 1896 from the High School. Their parents died and their uncles took them to England. At the sale of their personal goods Marshall Warren bought a chest with the date 1630 on it. The Gazette *household bought the brass andirons from the sale. Word came to Emporia the other day – to the J. Harvey Friths – that Jack Whitworth had been killed in action in the great drive in France on 26 March. He was a Major. But before he became a Major he had risen in civilian life. Twice he was defeated for Parliament as a Liberal. The obituary of him in his home paper in England says of him 'He returned to England with his eyes open and saw things which schoolboys seldom perceive - abject poverty and the drunkenness which thrives beside it.' That much life in a dry town had taught him to see. And he had the Kansas spirit, for the obituary notice proceeds 'He at once took an interest in reform, and an interest that was critical. It was thoroughly human. The essential democratic spirit of the West never deserted him. He was more than a champion of the poor. He made friendships with individual poor people, overlooking the accidents of life, and gripping the essentials.' That is Kansas for you.*

He was a member of his town council and a lawyer who served what corresponds to our free legal aid bureaus in the cities. When war came he got into it and worked up the line until he died a major. That's a pretty fine sort of life to live. And it's well worth while to think that the roots of that life were implanted here in Emporia, at our public schools, at the State Normal where the democratic life of this community so impressed a lad that when he was old he did not depart from it. His two uncles who took the Whitworth children were members of parliament and persons of means and consequence in their communities.'

His biography, *The Life of Major John Haworth Whitworth*, was written by his brother-in-law and old school friend, Revd. W.L. Mackennal, and published in Manchester in 1918. His sister, May, sent a copy of it to the J. Harvey Friths in Emporia and received back these letters:

Emporia, Kansas Feb 16th 1919

My dear Mary,
I received your letter and also the book the life of dear Jack for which I thank you for kindly remembering me with such a precious gift. I assure you dear May it was read with a great deal of interest by Mr. Frith and I, and shall now pass it on to the rest of the family and friends who knew you in Kansas. It brought back many pleasant memories of your life in the West. Even then we were prophesying great things for Jack. Had he lived no doubt he would have been one of England's rulers, but God must have some higher duty for him and his brother to perform. Blessed be the Will of God. While reading the book I was constantly reminded of your dear Mother and her life out here. How brave she was and never complaining. I shall never forget her kindness in those days, it meant a great deal to me. Her advice and sympathy which I found her always ready to give. For it I shall still love and cherish her memory. Now that the terrible war is over suppose you are getting settled down again. Gilbert didn't get to go over, his company was to sail the 12th. Nov. they went down to the docks in N. York when they were ordered back camp. He was dreadfully disappointed. He was home for Christmas. Mollie is home also from camp, she had the pneumonia but is getting stronger now. Alice and family are all well. Also Grace, Mr. Frith and Mollie join me in fond remembrance to all your family, thanking you once more for the book. Poor Jack he certainly had a full life.
With much love, Yours sincerely, M.B. Frith.

Emporia, Ks. Feb 16/19

My dear May,
It was with the keenest of sorrow that I heard of the deaths of your two brothers. It must however be of great comfort to you to reflect that a great honour has come to your family inasmuchas your dear brothers died fighting nobly for England.
With heartfelt sympathy, Very sincerely yours, J. Harvey Frith.

The best memorial to my grandfather was that given to the National Trust by the Fell and Rock Climbing Club of the English Lake District. In memory of twenty of their members killed during the First World War they purchased a good half of the highest parts of the central dome of mountains in the Lake District, in northern England, (some 3,000 acres), and presented it to the nation 'for the use and enjoyment of the people of our land for all time.' It includes a large part of Scafell, Scafell Pike,

179

Kirkfell, Base Brown, Brandreth, Green Gable, Glaramara, Great Gable and Great End, the Napes Needle, Kern Knotts, Lingmell, Esk Hause, Allen Crags and Seathwaite Fell. It was in these fells that he had spent many happy holidays walking and climbing with his friends from Oxford, and throughout his subsequent career. A bronze memorial plaque is placed on Great Gable.

Walter Haworth Whitworth 1882–1918

Nicholai Whitworth and Walter Whitworth in the Argentine

Walter Whitworth was the younger son of John and Marian Whitworth. When he returned to England in 1896 he went straight to Bowdon College with his elder brother to finish his schooling. From there he went on to Cirencester Agricultural College from which he graduated in 1905. He had his father's great love of the outdoor life, and as soon as he finished his training he decided to emigrate to Argentina. His choice of the Argentine may have been partly due to having some Whitworth cousins already established out there. Nicholai Whitworth, who as a young man had lived on the farm in Kansas and helped John Whitworth, was already established on an estancia near Buenos Aires, together with his sisters Annie, Kathleen and Constance. Annie Martha Whitworth was married to Ned Warren, who kept beef cattle in Argentina; their children were brought up by Irish relatives. Kathleen Whitworth married Henry W. Roberts whose firm H.W. Roberts and Co., an import/export business with ramifications in Nottingham, Manchester and Buenos Aires. Nicholai Whitworth had joined this firm in Buenos Aires. Walter set out for Argentina in 1905 and was soon established on the La Lornita Estancia at Berutti F.C.O. Life on the estancia was not very different from life on a farm in the Mid West: droughts and plagues of locusts are mentioned in the letters home, as also his large flock of sheep and crops of wheat and grass. In 1909 he travelled back to England for his sister Daisy's wedding.

In 1910 he married Nicholai Whitworth's sister, Constance (his cousin) in the Argentine, and their eldest son, John Nicholas Whitworth was born in Buenos Aires in January 1912. Their second son, Richard Haworth Whitworth was born in Nottingham in July 1913. Walter, like his father, was an excellent horseman, a good shot and a lover of sport of every kind. He was fond of adventure too and in his early days in Argentina explored parts of Patagonia where no other white man had ventured before. Walter's letters from the Argentine closely resemble his father's letters home from Kansas; here are extracts from several from 1907–1909 which give the flavour of life on an Argentine estancia.

Quiroga F.C.O. 22nd Oct 1907

My dear Daisy,
Many thanks for your letter. I was rather surprised to hear of your engagement to Robin; I am very glad you have picked out such a good man. He is a man after my own heart. I am sure you will make a happy pair. I congratulate you.

I am going to B/A tomorrow to see about my land. I am rather anxious as I have got the money out too late to pay on the day arranged and I am afraid of the seller backing out as the lands have been going up. I hope to arrange things satisfactorily. The family here are very interested in your engagement and join me in wishing you happiness.

Everything is looking blooming, the grass and wheat are growing apace and it looks as if Nick and Willie will do well this year, which I pray they will.

With much love, your affectionate brother, Walter.

La Lornita, Berutti F.C.O. 21st May 1908

My dear Daisy,
Many thanks for your letter. I am now working on my own place and have been herding my 750 sheep in the wet and rain for four days. Today it has turned out clear and frosty, I am glad to say, so that I will

have a chance of drying out my clothes. If you are much of a detective you will notice I have not got a table to write on. I am getting tired of spending money on things for the house, and am leading a simple quiet life.

My old Capataz from Salale is with me now. He has given up a job of £200 a year and is now working like a nigger for nothing (such is love). I am trying to get him a good job somewhere else.

Has Willie come to C.B.K. yet, and did he get you the rug I told him to? He is such a forgetful one.

I am riding into Berutti today to see if there are any letters from home. Has Gladys got engaged yet as she has not written anything about coming out recently?

When does your wedding come off? How I should like to be in England to see it.

I have an Italian and his wife working for me. The wife gives me more trouble than ten men: she is so stupid, and instead of sacking them I am so sorry for them that I cannot harden my heart and kick them out.

Hoping that all is going well with you and that the family are all well. Your affectionate brother, Walter.

Walter H. Whitworth Estancia 'La Lornita' Estancion Berutti F.C.O. 2nd Feb. 1909

My dear Daisy

I have cabled to say that I would come to England for your wedding (it is not every day that we have a wedding in the family). I propose leaving on the '*Athenie*' Shaw Saville, White Star Line, that is if I can get a berth. It leaves on 13th. April and ought to be in England for 7th. May. If you have made arrangements for before don't wait. I shall let you know later if I can get a berth. Things are beginning to look blooming again for me and I hope to have my house in order before I go home.

I was sorry to hear that your eyes have been giving you trouble, I hope you are taking good care of them now.

Love to yourself, Robin and family, Your affectionate brother, Walter.

'La Lornita', Berutti F.C.O. *(undated, 1910)*

My dear Daisy,

Many thanks for your kind letter of the 7th. January and for your good wishes. We have been passing through a rather rough time what with locusts, drought and the other five plagues of Egypt, but now the tide has turned and it looks as if a prosperous time was coming.

I have been entertaining furiously lately. Mrs. Barrington and her mother Mrs. Oyler have been stopping here two days, making my curtains for me – don't you think it good of them? McMorran is also stopping with me as he is going to Ireland soon.

I enclose a photo of wee brother on a pony he trained and gave to Mrs. Barrington last Xmas – one of the best ponies I ever was on. Look at the young tree behind the horse – it is a white stick now. The locusts have peeled it.

I wonder if you have seen Nick, he ought to be returning soon. Poor old chap he has always been 'up against it' as we say in America.

May writes me rabid radical letters. Politics seem to get on the brain. I am going to tell her that I have met quite a lot of good, honest Conservatives on my travels. I am sorry that Jack did not have a walk over – Next time he will have better luck I hope. I see in your letter you are expecting a new arrival – you have my very best wishes and sympathy during the troublesome time. Please give Robin my love – Now that I have curtains I shall be expecting you and Robin to come out and visit me, if not this year, next.

Remember me to Mr and Mrs Thew and with best love and wishes to yourself,

Your affectionate brother, Walter.

His estancia prospered and he specialised in stock-raising and horsebreaking with success, and he had a happy young family. With the outbreak of war his thoughts turned to England and how he could lend a hand. In a letter to his brother, Jack, dated 25th August 1914 he wrote: 'I am practising shooting every day and hope and pray that by the middle of November to be able to come home and offer my services as one who can shoot and ride. Connie is with me and is willing that we travel second class and that she and the kids take a cheap cottage somewhere in England. I know a good man who can look after the place while I am away and I can trust my neighbours ...' To his sister, May, he wrote in September 1914 'If my financial position did not need my undivided efforts I should be at the Front and Connie at the head of a regiment of nurses.' Despite many difficulties – he was at first rejected because of serious heart trouble – he eventually joined the Lancashire Fusiliers as a second Lieutenant. At Christmas 1917 he saw his brother, Jack, who was on leave from his regiment in France. At this time Walter was a private in the

Artists Rifles O.T.C. His family were by now staying in England with the Roberts family at Cliff House, Radcliffe-on-Trent, Notts. Walter was sent to the Front towards the end of August 1918 and wrote to his family: 'Well, I could not stick in the Argentine and let all these fine men fight for me. I fully appreciate the horrors of war, and would not have come home if I could have reconciled my conscience and my honour to keeping out of it.' He was particularly sensitive to the suffering of others and only his closest friends and relations knew what it meant to him to face the horrors of the battlefield. It was thus particularly sad that he died on 14th September 1918 of wounds received in battle the previous day, only three weeks after going to the front, and so shortly before the end of the war, at the age of 36. He was buried at the Heath Cemetery, Harbonnières, Somme.

Walter Whitworth in military uniform

The Whitworth family's nanny, Nellie Kirkpatrick, *née* Clark, who had helped Marian Whitworth with her young family in Bowdon before they went out to Emporia, wrote as follows on hearing of Walter's death:

Keating P.O., B.C., Canada Nov. 3 1918

My dear May

I am so very sorry to hear about your dear brother Walter's death. Poor, dear, brave boy to come all those thousands of miles to be killed. But when he looked at it as his duty he could not do otherwise.

When I think of the beautiful baby he was and how much love and care he needed to keep him, he was a very frail baby when born and your mother and myself had many anxious times until he was about six months old then after that he gained strength, but he never was a strong, robust boy. We always said he was like china. Still he turned out a fine man. You must try and find comfort as you say in being able to have him near you and know him better this last year... I am so proud of my two dear boys, the life they have led and the good they have been able to do. How proud your father and mother would have been of them ...

With very much love, I remain your affectionate friend, Nellie Kirkpatrick.

Memorial windows to John and Walter Whitworth were placed in the porch of Bowdon Downs Congregational Church, where they are commemorated with other members of the congregation who gave their lives for the nation in the Great War.

Mary (May) Whitworth 1878–1967

When the young Whitworth family returned to England from Emporia it was May who kept house for them all at Church Bank, Bowdon. It was probably May who most felt the full impact of the tragic end of the Emporia chapter in the Whitworth family saga. She was the only member of the family old enough to sign the legal documents about the sale of the farm and its contents, and it was to her that all the details of the final American transactions were sent by her uncle, Jesse Haworth.

The atmosphere of life at Church Bank is charmingly evoked by this poem written by Constance Whitworth for May's autograph book in 1901:

In memory of the summer of 1901

I am sitting sadly thinking
Of the summer almost past
Of the cycling, boating, tennis,
And the teas upon the grass,
Of 'coffee pots' and gardens,
The faint smell of cigarettes,
And many funny dances –
These are things one can't forget.

I am thinking of the steamer
On which the boys depart
And the girls they leave together
All a breaking of their hearts -
Of speech-making at Church Bank
And of some smiling snap,
And the general opinion
We wish the boys were back.

I am sitting idly thinking
Of the summer almost past
And my hopeful heart keeps saying
That it will not be the last.
We'll have a good time again May
In a summer yet to come
So keep a bright look out until
The winter days are done.

May's whole life's interest centred round the family and the welfare of her brothers and sisters. She and her sisters helped Jack with his election campaigns in Shrewsbury and Knutsford. She kept in touch with some Emporia friends, notably the J. Harvey Frith family, and she received occasional postcards from Maggie Falconer. In November 1908 she received the following message on a picture postcard of the post office in Emporia: 'Boss said when you write to Walter ask him if he wont send us two or three postcards from where he is. We would be glad to get them. M. F. (Mrs. Frith).' Gradually her brothers and sisters left home and got married. She never married. During the First War she became a Red Cross Nurse. It was a tremendous blow to her when in 1918 she lost both her brothers, and it was probably this, together with the earlier tragedy which made her subject to depressions and unnecessary worry about everyday financial matters. She was very close to her sisters, and devoted to her brothers' families. During the war she used to stay with Gladys and William MacKennal at Compton Martin, near Bristol. After they moved to Chesterton, Cambridge, in 1920, she bought a house close to them at 2, Leys Road, Cambridge. Here she lived happily for nearly ten years, until the MacKennals moved north to Kirkby Lonsdale. In 1933 she decided to settle at Hightown near Liverpool, close to her other sister, Daisy, who lived at Blundellsands, and also to Constance Whitworth, Walter's widow, and two sons who she saw frequently.

She did not find it easy to make friends, but was good with children and loved keeping in touch with all the family. She was extremely houseproud, and, like her sisters, was interested in collecting china.

Cecily Marguerite (Daisy) Whitworth (Mrs Robin Thew) 1881–1960

Daisy was considered to be very pretty, and there was some amusement in the family when one of her suitors inquired if 'Miss Whitworth was bespoke.' Her brothers and sisters did not think very much of her cooking, and dreaded when it was her turn to prepare the meals; rice pudding was served every day and even though she was good at cooking it long and slow, it did become rather monotonous. She married Henry Arthur (Robin) Thew in 1909. He was an Oxford friend of her brother Jack; they both went up to Wadham in 1898, and had lodgings in the same house, they both read law and shared Liberal political interests. They were close friends and spent much of their time discussing legal points and problems.

Writing to Robin in February 1908, before they were married, Daisy told him 'we have one volume of Our Mutual Friend, the other was burnt in America.' Thus the impact of the fire of 1886 lived on.

After Oxford Robin Thew joined his uncle's firm and became a partner in Avison, Morton, Paxton and Co., solicitors of 5, Cook St., Liverpool. He had been born in Scotland in 1879 of a family with Huguenot ancestry. He was lame all his life as a result of a babyhood accident, and spent his childhood on his back in a long wheelchair and later on crutches. He had no formal schooling but was taught at home by a tutor. Robin's greatest interest was in music and he became chairman of the Liverpool Philharmonic Society. Although in constant pain, he seldom complained, and had a wonderful sense of humour much enjoyed by his family and friends.

Daisy and Robin had two children; Henry Whitworth Thew born in 1910, and Marian Milnes Thew (later Campin) born in 1914. They lived at Newlands, Blundellsands near Liverpool. Daisy was a splendid homemaker and mother. She became an expert wood carver, crochet lace maker and embroideress. She was a sincere teetotaller and Congregationalist and in 1924 became a Christian Scientist which she remained until her death in 1960. As a young woman she went to Switzerland with her sister, May, and won cups for bob-sleighing at winter sports. Daisy and Robin had a splendid holiday home in the Yorkshire dales: Battlehill, Austwick, a very old cottage which was much enjoyed by many members of the family.

Gladys Hope Whitworth (MacKennal) 1884–1979

Gladys was the youngest child of John and Marian Whitworth. She was born just a month before her father left for America. Most of her earliest memories were of life on the farm near Emporia, where she was taken at the age of two. She loved the freedom of life on the prairie, and remembered with great pleasure the fun she and Walter had playing in the timber, or down by the river, or on the farm. She adored her mother, and when her mother was ill she used to sit on her mother's bed after the doctor's visits. Her mother was much respected in the neighbourhood and she remembered several occasions when neighbours came in for meals. One neighbour, Mr. Alexander, who had once been a slave, did not know how to use cutlery, and her mother taught him these skills quietly without making any fuss. She remembered how they always said Grace before meals, and how they used to go into Emporia to the Congregational Church for services on Sundays, or, occasionally to the Plumb Creek Sunday School, and how her father had preached a sermon there. Her eldest sister, May, and brother John (Jack) had ridden from the farm to school in Emporia every day, some four miles away. She also recalled that they had visitors from England to help on the farm – both relations and others.

On returning to England she went to boarding school in Harrogate, Yorkshire and afterwards, with her cousin, Isabel Boyd, to a domestic science training college at Colwall near Malvern, Worcestershire (now called St. James' College). She was bright and intelligent and an excellent cook.

When her brother, Walter, emigrated to Argentina she undertook the three week voyage from Southampton to Buenos Aires to spend six months with him on his estancia. Before she left the Revd William Mackennal had made her a proposal of marriage. He had to wait till her return from the Argentine for her acceptance. William Mackennal was the son of the Revd. Alexander Mackennal, for many years the pastor of Bowdon Downs Congregational Chapel, who had taken part in the wedding of John and Marian Whitworth in 1877. William was a lifelong friend of Gladys' brother, Jack. They had been at school together in Bowdon before the Whitworths had gone to Kansas, and he was to write Jack's biography in 1919. At the time of their wedding in 1913 William was curate at St. James' church, Grimsby, and later (1914) became Rector of Compton Martin near Bristol. They were here during the fateful year of 1918 when both Gladys' brothers were killed. In 1920 William was appointed Vicar of St. Andrew's, Chesterton, Cambridge. He was no stranger to Cambridge having read History at Trinity College, graduating in 1906. He had been ordained deacon in 1907, and priest in 1908 by the Bishop of Ely, and was curate at Great St. Mary's Church from 1907 under Archdeacon Cunningham. In 1908 he was appointed chaplain and lecturer at Westcott House theological college in Cambridge.

They spent fourteen happy years at Chesterton before moving to Kirkby Lonsdale, Westmorland, (a Trinity College living), and three years later to another Trinity living at St. Mary's, Hitchen. In 1942 William became Archdeacon of Ely and they moved back to Boxmoor Cottage, 36, Arbury Road, Cambridge which was to be their final home. They had no children.

Gladys was a great support to her husband in his ministry. She often drove her husband to meetings and services; she enjoyed playing golf with him, and loved travelling - to Morocco, Florence, the Alps, the Yorkshire dales and the Lake District. She was a keen gardener and an assiduous collector of fine porcelain.

Above all she will be remembered as a charming hostess to many generations of undergraduates who recall with gratitude her warm interest in their affairs, her delightful sense of humour, and independence of mind. Her husband died in 1947 but she lived on in Cambridge for another 32 years, dying in Bath after a few months' illness on 1st May 1979. She was tremendously proud of living to be over 90, and to a greater age than any other member of her immediate family. In 1942 she had an unexpected contact with Emporia. She was listening to the radio when, to her astonishment, she heard an interview with William Allen White, the editor and owner of the Emporia Gazette. She wrote to him at once.

Dear Mr. White,

It was particularly interesting to me to listen to your words on the BBC this afternoon because I lived on a farm four miles from Emporia from 1886 to 1896. My father and mother, John and Marian Whitworth are buried in Emporia. My two sisters are still alive. My elder brother, John Haworth Whitworth, who began his education at the State Normal and proceeded to Oxford University, England, after winning the D.S.O. and M.C. was killed in the offensive which began on 21st. March 1918. My younger brother, Walter, was also killed in the war. His son John is a Wing Commander in the R.A.F. and has won the D.S.O., D.F.C., and Bar. He was one of six airmen sent by the British Government to the States a few months ago and made a point of flying over Emporia.

Little did I think in those far off times that I should one day listen in my home in England to the voice of one of Emporia's leading citizens.

Yours truly, Gladys Mackennal.

She received the following reply:

Emporia Gazette, Emporia, Kansas April 18th 1942

Dear Mrs Mackennal,

I must have known you as a young girl. Mrs. White and I came here in 1895 and we remember the Whitworths very well. I remember a pretty, young, darkhaired girl who might have been you, and I remember when death shattered your family and you went to live in England. You left many things here. An old oak chest that carried the name of Mary Bore or Bohr was sold at auction and a neighbour bought it. We bought the brass andirons with lovely knobs. We gave them to our son, Bill, who still uses them.

It is odd that you should have heard my voice over the BBC and I am proud and happy that you thought it worthwhile to write me a letter.

With kind regards. I am most cordially yours, W.A. White.*

The *Emporia Gazette* 10th April 1942 recorded this correspondence in an article entitled

Voice Across the world

A few weeks ago an agent of the British Broadcasting Company came to Emporia with a record making machine and took a 15 minute phonograph record interview from the Editor of the Emporia Gazette for distribution over the British Broadcasting Company in England and the British Empire, whereupon everyone around the office forgot it. Today a letter dropped into the office from the Church House, Cambridge, England. The letter was signed by Gladys Whitworth Mackennal, wife of the Archdeacon of Ely. Gladys Whitworth lived out on Sixth Avenue 44 years ago. (Then follows an account of the letter) ...

The miracle of the voice recorded here in the Gazette Office seeking out the ears of a woman who was a little girl in Emporia is one of those wonders which has in it the destiny of man, good or evil. The flying machine which took a grandson from England across this town to look down upon the graves of his grandparents lying in our graveyard, was another thing, so strange in the long thousands of years that man has been on this planet that our generation, rushed into all these wonders, is baffled, bewildered, and may be misguided. God only knows.

* William Allen White (1868–1944) was a famous American newspaper editor and author. In 1895 he borrowed $3,000 and bought the Emporia Gazette which he edited and published for the rest of his life. Through its columns he became known throughout the United States as the 'Sage of Emporia'; it revealed him as a genial and warm-hearted journalist who reflected the attitudes of the middle-class in the Mid West. He won two Pulitzer prizes for his writings. He died in Emporia in January 1944.

Helen Whitworth (Mrs Leo Rogers) 1870–1953

Helen Whitworth was the eldest daughter of Thomas Whitworth and his wife Elizabeth *née* Shaw. (Thomas was John Whitworth's elder brother, who stayed in the cotton trade when John emigrated to America in 1884). They had seven children: Arthur, Helen, Florence, Ethel, Alice, Thomas and Hilda. Helen went out to Emporia to help her uncle and his children when Marian Whitworth died in 1894. She found herself landed with the considerable task of winding up the estate and bringing the family home after the accidental death of her uncle in 1896, as the letters show.

On her return to England she rejoined her family at Waterloo, near Liverpool. She was restless and soon began to plan a return to America, but other events intervened as this letter from her china-painting teacher and friend, Mrs Anna W. Graham of Emporia, reveals.

Emporia, Kansas. March 20th. 1898

My dear Helen,

Your very welcome letter came last Tuesday, followed this week by the gloves. Let me thank you for the latter as they are very lovely and I am now in the state where new ones are a necessity. I am going to try them on today and I am sure they will fit, then too they are such a nice colour.

Now for the letter. You cannot imagine how delighted I was to read of your engagement and I most truly hope you may be very happy in the venture. Mr. Rogers is surely a lucky fellow and I hope he appreciates the fact. My best wish is that you may be as truly happy as I have been in my married life. Truly two people could not be better mated than we have been and I trust you may also be as fortunate. I am so glad you are so happy now and can really quite easily give up the fact that you are not coming back to the us in the States again – though I did not think anything

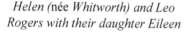

Helen (née Whitworth) and Leo Rogers with their daughter Eileen

Mr and Mrs John Graham of Emporia

could reconcile me to that. John said I was as excited as if I'd been engaged over again, so you see I really was pleased, as to Mr. Rogers I am going to write to him a bit of a note in this which I want you to forward to him if you will, please. I do hope sometime the Vancouver farm will bring you over here again, that I may have a peep at you, though I hate to think of you having more ' farm' life, so I trust the Manchester business may thrive. Joy be with you my dear friend in this venture and may your cup of it be filled to the brim. You must write me fully of your plans and anticipations for you know I shall be interested even in the smallest detail. Don't have a long engagement, my dear girl, for no matter how long you are engaged you will have to become acquainted all over again in another way when you are married – and there is so much pleasure in one's own home. I do not want you to delay longer than necessary. I am full to the fingertips with interest in it all and do wish I could talk it over with you. It is quite surprising weather here, not as bad a March as usual, and I trust our winter is over. All the flowers are starting out quite nicely and I so much enjoy seeing them come forth …

We have had such a grief in the death of Mr. Amett – he has been sick so long of Bright's disease, nearly a year – a month ago his mind failed and he became raving – jumping out of the window and running off in all kinds of weather, clothed or not, by day or night. Through it all he had the greatest liking for John who could always quiet him … he ran many times to the store for his 'protection' as he thought …

The Congregational Church is to have a convention this week, and Wed. night they give a supper to the delegates. I am to help serve so I shall be busy I know. I have felt so mean lately. we have been under such a strain with Mr. A's illness, that we have not attempted even church going of late – so will have to get into harness again I suppose …

I have been busy with my needle lately doing a sofa pillow and a yellow centre piece … Could I send you a piece of fancy work in a paper sometime? You know more whether it would go through or not. I know you said Uncle Sam was quite particular about things going your way. What is the best way to get them through? How I should love to do you a little bit occasionally. We have had cooking school again this week by Miss Andrews and I have some nice recipes should you care for any American cooking in your new home …

We have some fine Kansas mud again, you know what that means, don't you. I do not see Mr. Falconer* at all any more, nor hear of him. Mr. Jones in Newman's always enquires after you most kindly, and speaks so nicely of your Uncle John and his wife. I am going out to the cemetery with the first bunch of flowers that come out, for it does me good to leave a posy there when all belonging are so far away. Has Walter reconciled himself to being in England yet? … Do you see much of Mr. Rogers, and does he now live in Manchester? I suppose if so, letters are frequent anyway.

Do not put yourself out the least bit about the painted flowers, for you know any time will do for me and I don't want you to inconvenience yourself one bit. I must close now … Our best wishes and blessings to you during your engagement and may your marriage be full of many happy things. a kiss, my dear Helen, in this new joy. My best regards to the children when you next write to them.

With much love from your Kansas friend, Anna W. Graham

* *Walter H. Falconer and his wife Margaret (Maggie) lived at 201, South Congress St., Emporia after their marriage in May 1895. He worked as bookkeeper for the City Roller Mill (Teichgraber Mill), and for the Newton Brother's Garage. He died in April 1944, just two years after his wife. They had one daughter, Mary Elizabeth Yearout of Portland, Oregon. (Emporia Gazette, 24 April 1944: Lyon County Historical Society, Emporia)*

Helen Whitworth married Leo Rogers in 1898, so their engagement was not a long one. They had met in the house of mutual friends, the Hollingers, at Old Trafford, Manchester. Leo was twelve or fourteen years older than Helen. He was the son of Thomas Rogers of Oldham Road, Manchester, a cabinet maker, pawnbroker, and keen amateur botanist, who had been born in Oldham but came from a Welsh family. He died on Helvellyn in the Lake District and is buried in Patterdale churchyard.

Leo Rogers as a young man went out to Canada to work on the Canadian Pacific Railway. He settled in Vancouver where he had a log cabin and farm. He damaged his knee in an accident with a horse on his farm, which left him with a permanent stiffness.

Helen had been planning to return to America to work with a family in New York, but her marriage changed that plan. After their wedding they lived at Chorlton-cum-Hardy and later moved to Heaton Moor near Stockport, and eventually to Hale in Cheshire. Leo Rogers became a jeweller in Manchester. He was agent for Waltham Watches from America, and also was a specialist in diamonds. His trade prospered so he did not return to Vancouver. Helen and Leo had a daughter, Eileen, who was born in 1901. It was Eileen Rogers who had inherited and carefully kept the larger part of this collection of Whitworth letters from Emporia, together with other family papers which form the basis for this book.

Helen kept in touch with the Grahams in Kansas until they died in the 1940s: she received photographs and paintings from Mrs. Graham, and news of friends in Emporia. Unfortunately she was unable to keep up her china painting, although I have the handsome set of Limoges plates which she painted in Emporia.

Helen kept in close touch with her young Whitworth cousins whom she had brought back from Kansas. When Jack set off for France in 1917, he wrote to her as follows:

4/3/17

Dear Helen,

We are just off to France tonight ready to do our little bit. I was sorry not to be able to come round and say goodbye when I was home on leave. I hope this summer will see it through and that we shall soon be living our ordinary lives again.

Kindest regards to Mr. Rogers and Eileen, Yours affectionately, J.H. Whitworth.

He wrote to her again later that year from France:

16/11/17

Dear Helen,

Many thanks for the cake which arrived safely and has been much appreciated. At the present moment we are in support a fair distance behind the line. I am at the present moment a Major, but as a new second-in-command is coming out I shall revert to Captain in a few days. I may be sent behind the lines to train Americans which will be quite a good stunt. I hope you are keeping better. Please remember me to Mr. Rogers and Eileen,

With love, Yours ever, J.H. Whitworth.

Helen must have felt the deaths of John and Walter in France in 1918 almost as much as their sisters did. After John died she wrote to May:

62, Westgate, Hale April 11th. 1918

My dear May,

I thank you and Ida for sending me John's two letters. May I keep them for a few days? He writes so cheerfully, and in such hope of seeing his dear ones. I cannot but think the end must have come suddenly, thus he would be spared the anguish of knowing he was leaving you all. I do hope Ida has further particulars by this time. The loss is terrible enough without it being added to by this long suspense … I keep thinking of many incidents of our life together, and sometime I will write to Kansas and have John's name added on the stone there. I know Mrs. Graham would see to it for us. Leo and Eileen join me in loving messages to Ida and with love to yourself,

Yours lovingly, Helen.

Nicholas Martyn (Nicholai) Whitworth 1871–1936

Nicholai joined his cousin John Whitworth on the farm near Emporia towards the end of 1886 and stayed with the family through the trauma of the fire, eventually leaving in March 1888. He was the elder son of 'old'

Nicholai Whitworth (born at Nicholiev in Russia in 1844) and Martha ('Polly') Stone, daughter of Dr Joseph Stone of Drogheda. His grandfather was William Whitworth who was an engineer, had built lighthouses on the Caspian and Black Sea, was inturned during the Crimean War; later he settled in Drogheda and became resident partner of the Whitworth Brothers' cotton mills, and MP for Newry. Nicholai's father, 'old' Nicholas, succeeded William Whitworth as the manager of the Drogheda mills.

It is not clear what happened to 'young' Nicholai after he left Kansas, but his sisters Annie, Kathleen and Constance as well as his brothers William (Willie) and Benjamin all went out to the Argentine, and he was in Buenos Aires by 1891. Annie Martha was married to Ned Warren, a beef cattle farmer; Kathleen was married to Henry Roberts who had an import/export business between the Argentine and England, and Constance was to marry (in 1910) her cousin Walter Haworth Whitworth, the youngest son of John and Marian, who had emigrated to Argentina in 1905. Nicholai Whitworth never married. He seems to have had bad luck with his farming, but he managed to get back to England from time to time to see the rest of the family. He was back in 1901 and gave his cousin May a commonplace book in which he wrote 'When far away from ye/ in South Amerikee/ still dear to me will be/ my thoughts of all of ye. Nick. Sale June 26/01 day before sailing and my birthday.' He wrote to his cousin May:

31, Esmerelda, Buenos Aires Octr. 14/02

My dear May,

I was so pleased to get your letter and two photos today, for which very many thanks, and I will reciprocate shortly with mine – if the camera doesn't break, as some day this week or next I shall have to sit down to the ordeal of the photographer, as I did the dentist the other day.

I am glad to hear that Con looks well, for the poor girl gets badly treated, but I can't help it for she knows very well that if I could afford to be a more generous brother, I would. I sent her a £5 note the other day for her birthday – and as trade has revived a lot that was no sacrifice. I spend money on myself and others out here which probably I oughtn't to, but I have a position to keep up, which makes otherwise unnecessary demands.

You must have had a poor summer for cycling etc., while here we have had no rain for two, nearly three months. But a change came and just enough rain fell to let us know rain comes from the skies, for clouds we seldom see.

I had such a lovely 10 days holiday this year, for I went with two friends, officers of H.M.S. '*Cambrian*', to the estancia Willie is managing, and also to another one 15 miles away, where we had some grand sport. We shot deer, ostrich, swan, geese, duck, chimangos – large hawks, Martinetas – tailless pheasants, partridge, snipe, and one or two waterhens by mistake when firing at ducks … Annie was staying with Willie and so we had a great family gathering – 3 Whitworths or half one family – with Ben not very far away …

I was sorry to hear of the death of Mr. Haworth,* who always had a kind word for me – tho' somehow he used to let me know that I was a Whitworth and the Whitworths owed him money. I should very much have liked to have seen him since the estate (*in Kansas*) has been wound up, paying in full – for he would not have to say anything more about it. For altho' I had no responsibility, I always felt I was an abandoned lump of humanity – doing my best to work for my Father's and Mother's and Con's sake – never my own – without a word – let alone practical help from a solitary friend, except Mr. Edmund Whitworth, and Mr. James Stuart.

Well May, this is gruesome reading but true. I must get to work – and many thanks for the two good photos, and love to you all,

Your affectionate Nick.

* *Mr Abraham Haworth died in Hyères, southern France, in March 1902. He was the elder brother of Marian Whitworth, née Haworth. His career had been spent in the firm of John Dilworth and Son, cotton yarn spinners, of which he eventually became the head. He was a familiar figure at the Manchester Royal Exchange. He was also interested in education, had supported the foundation of Mansfield College, Oxford, and was a governor of Manchester Grammar School. He is described as being a kindly upright man and a thoughtful counsellor to his business associates and friends. He collected paintings of such artists as Copley Fielding, Cox, Turner, Holman Hunt and Briton Rivière. His wife was Elizabeth née Goodier who died in 1900.*

An Argentine newspaper reported the following in late 1930:

On 27 November 1930 Nicholas Whitworth of 'El Cuaparote', Hereford, F.C.O. noticed a score of hawks, 'aguilluz' had come to roost in his garden. In order to frighten them off before they could attack his chickens, he shot them killing four birds. One of them was wearing a red celluloid ring inscribed '50 Canada'. This bird was a Swainson's hawk which had been ringed in 1929 by Glen and Jack Scherdfager of Halkirk, Alberta. This was the first record of a Swainson's hawk being banded in Canada and recovered in South America.

Nicholai Whitworth died at Cuenca, Argentina 11th April 1936. In his last years he had been very distressed by his sister Kathleen's attitude to the rest of the family. She was clearly rather disturbed, and dwelt on her troubles, real or imagined. She had refused to see her sister Constance, had upset him on his last trip home, had fallen out with her husband, Henry Roberts, and refused to answer letters from the family in the Argentine. He was buried at Llavallah in the same cemetery as his brother, Willie.

The fate of the Whitworth Farm near Emporia, Kansas

The Gilson newspaper clipping scrapbook at the Lyon County Historical Museum in Emporia has the following entries about the stone house built by John Whitworth in 1887, under the heading Korte.

12.8.1947

Korte Farm House, a Lyon County Landmark, is destroyed by fire.

An old rock house built many years ago by an immigrant English family is in ruins now as a result of the fire that occurred in the middle of the night. The house is on the Korte Brothers farm, four and a half miles east and one and a half miles north of the town, and for the past 60 years had been owned by the Korte family. The fire was discovered by Henry Korte about 1.30 o'clock Thursday morning. The flames had made such headway that Mr. Korte was barely able to escape from the house and was unable to save any of his possessions. The Korte House was acquired more than 60 years ago by the late Henry Korte, father of the present Henry Korte, and was a well-known landmark. It was located on a 320 acre grain and stock farm.

Recalls history of Korte Farm House, built by an Englishman

The Korte House east of town, which burned early Thursday morning has an interesting history. This is the second house to burn on this farm. The farm one time in the '70s was owned and occupied by the late Col. H.C. Whitley. It was sold to a man by the name of Whitworth who came here from England. The house stood on a knoll across the river from the highway near the Neosho river bridge ... The house was built of stone with a basement, two full stories and a finished attic. The large dining room, with its double doors was connected to the parlour. Across the long entrance hall (a staircase) led to the second storey where there were five bedrooms. The woodwork throughout was walnut ... In 1896 the house

*Three views of the ruins of the Whitworth
farm after the fire, December 1947*

*was bought by Henry Korte who with his wife, two daughters and four
sons came here from Louisville, Kentucky ... William and Henry Korte, the
youngest sons never married and had lived for many years in the big
house with its stately, high-ceilinged rooms.*

When I met Robert Korte (the nephew of William and Henry Korte) in
Emporia in 1984, he told me that the house had been much neglected by
his uncles prior to the fire in 1947, and he remembered seeing large
cracks in the masonry of the outside walls. Mrs. Norma Redeker, a
granddaughter of Henry Korte, whose mother had grown up on the farm,
described it in a letter to me (April 1983): 'It was a unique house for
Kansas at that time. It had a bathroom, a copper tub and a pump over the
tub. The house also had two pantries.' When my husband and I visited
the site of the farm in April 1984 there was only a pile of rubble to mark
where the house had been. The only part of the farm which survived was
the old wind pump.

It would no doubt have given John and Marian Whitworth great
satisfaction to know that their five children had given rise to eight
grandchildren, eleven great-grandchildren, and twenty great-great-
grandchildren, and the first few of the next generation of great-great-
great-grandchildren, as shown in the final family tree.

199

In Gladys Whitworth's autograph album, given to her by her elder brother, Jack Whitworth, at Christmas 1899, he wrote the following starred verses from this poem by Longfellow which is here quoted in full to make an appropriate ending to this episode in the Whitworth family history.

A Psalm of Life
What the heart of the young man said to the psalmist

Tell me not in mournful numbers,
'Life is but an empty dream!'
For the soul is dead that slumbers,
And things are not what they seem.

Life is real! Life is earnest!
And the grave is not its goal;
'Dust thou art, to dust returnest,'
Was not spoken to the soul.

Not enjoyment, and not sorrow,
Is our destined end or way;
But to act, that each tomorrow
Finds us farther than today.

Art is long, and Time is fleeting,
And our hearts, though stout and brave,
Still, like muffled drums, are beating
Funeral marches to the grave.

* In the World's broad field of battle
In the bivouac of Life
Be not like driven cattle!
Be a hero in the strife!

* Trust no Future, however pleasant!
Let the dead Past bury its dead!
Act, act in the living Present!
Heart within and God o'erhead!

Lives of great men all remind us
We can make our lives sublime,
And, departing, leave behind us
Footprints in the sands of time;-

Footprints, that perhaps another,
Sailing o'er Life's solemn main,
A forlorn and shipwrecked brother,
Seeing, shall take heart again.

Let us, then, be up and doing,
With a heart for any fate;
Still achieving, still pursuing,
Learn to labour and to wait.

H.W. Longfellow (1807–1882)

The Descendants of John and Marian Whitworth of Emporia, Kansas

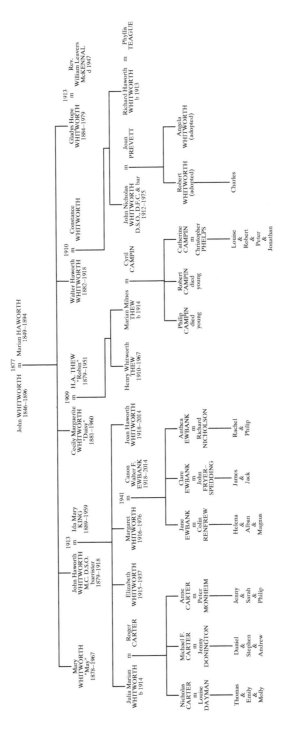

Lightning Source UK Ltd.
Milton Keynes UK
UKHW021122221221
396033UK00006B/50